# *Y*earning for Home
## in Troubled Times

# $\mathcal{Y}$earning for Home
## in Troubled Times

## Kenwyn K. Smith

THE
PILGRIM
PRESS
Cleveland

*For Sara, Justin, Phillip, and Kalila*

The Pilgrim Press
700 Prospect Avenue East
Cleveland, Ohio 44115-1100
pilgrimpress.com

© 2003 by The Pilgrim Press

Published 2003

Printed in the United States of America on acid-free paper

08   07   06   05   04   03            5   4   3   2   1

**Library of Congress Cataloging-in-Publication Data**
Smith, Kenwyn K.
    Yearning for home in troubled times / Kenwyn K. Smith.
        p.   cm.
    Includes bibliographical references.
    ISBN 0-8298-1536-8 (pbk. : alk. paper)
    1. Spiritual life. 2. Homelessness – Religious aspects.   I. Title.
BL624 .S5948 2003
302.3′4 – dc21
                                                        2002035470

# Contents

# Preface

What powerful pictures have been embossed on our hearts in recent decades: refugees fleeing the political instability of their homeland; hordes of former enemies dancing together in the streets as the Berlin Wall collapsed; starving children rushing toward relief workers bringing a truckload of food to the famine-stricken; power being peacefully transferred from the apartheid regime to a South African man who had been a political prisoner for twenty-seven years; innocents being gassed or gunned down by the armed forces of a dictator indifferent to the plight of the populace; a man wearing sandals and a loincloth walking the length and breadth of India announcing to the world that the end of colonialism was at hand; New Yorkers combing the streets and asking strangers, "Have you seen my daddy? my daughter? my best friend?" an African American preacher standing on the steps of the Lincoln Memorial telling the world, "I have a dream." The list is long, the stories exceedingly touching — pain and exhilaration, tears and laughter, sadness and ecstasy side by side.

Life is full of ironies. When the desecrated is replaced by decency and civility we are bold enough to believe that a new dawn has broken. Yet within a few years we often face dynamics as troublesome as those they replaced. My generation grew up with the Cold War and wondered if we would even reach midlife, so it seemed miraculous when former enemies became allies, old hatreds vanished, and new life appeared in places where the human spirit appeared to be dead. But the next decade brought a plethora of ethnic wars, suicide bombers, and new oppressors occupying the seats of those they had displaced in the name of liberty. How painfully reality mocks our dreams!

There was once a time when the plight or well-being of the people in any part of the world was contained within that region. Those days have gone. Along with the globalization of business, with all its plusses and minuses, has come the globalization of the human condition, with all its ups and downs. The predicaments of the displaced in Serbia or Bangladesh can be rapidly exported to the refugee camps of a nation on the other side of the world. A change in the interest rates of a large country can rescue or destroy a tottering economy in a small nation. Foot and mouth disease, environmental contamination, and AIDS refuse to respect geographic boundaries. Local disputes can become internationalized in a heartbeat, and foreign intervention can help sustain a troubled land.

Today, most conversations around the dinner table, in the coffee shop, on the train, at the water cooler, in the community center, at the local pub are based on three existential questions: How is humanity going to find a new way to live? Is there no place on earth where one can feel safe? What are we going to do with our vulnerability? Once wealth and military might enabled some to feel safe. But those days have passed. The illusion of invulnerability has been blown away for everyone. Even the privileged have been catapulted into an emotional world where the ever-present companions are anxiety, suspicion, and uncertainty about whether loved ones will return home safely at day's end. How does one live with such toxic fear? What form of sociopolitical evolution must occur for all to survive, let alone thrive, with our full humanity intact?

In the United States three social problems stand out as bold indicators of the collective need to evolve to a new level: drug dependency, homelessness, and mental health. With each passing decade these social ills become more intractable — despite the war on drugs, the proliferation of rehab programs, the billions pumped into the mental health profession, the creation of wonder drugs, deinstitutionalization, homeless shelters, Habitat for Humanity, and low-cost housing loans for the poor. So many resources have been dedicated to getting rid of these social problems, yet they grow in magnitude and complexity with the passing years.

Perhaps it is time to develop a different approach. The American Dream has long upheld virtues such as the pursuit of wealth, freedom from harm, and religious liberty. When threatened, the system tries to restore normalcy; and it relies on these core values to guide the restoration efforts. But could it be that the wish to accumulate more and more has become a national addiction? That the yearning for a life without vulnerability is a defense against spiritual truths that can be learned only by the exposed heart? That excessive dependency upon dogma, be it fundamentalist or libertarian, is a form of religious enslavement? And that mental health programs have been made into a commodity to be bought and sold in the social service marketplace? The knotted ball of yarn now wrapped around our self-evident truths has made reality so entwined that often the solution creates the problem that demands the solution that creates the problem, etc.

What is the way out? Maybe those caught in the repetitive cycles of failure hold the clue. Members of twelve-step programs know that trying to drive personal vulnerability underground guarantees a return to the abyss, so those in recovery try to live with their precariousness visible. Psychotherapists help patients to open up the closed heart, to release unwanted emotions once driven away. And each day the homeless live with the uncertainty of where the next meal will come from or where to lay their heads at nightfall. Could it be that these at-risk populations have, in their own quiet ways, been preparing us to learn what we have collectively been reluctant to absorb: that we are all vulnerable all the time, even those trying never to feel the aches of the exposed heart.

The times have changed. Even the strong and wealthy have lost their illusion of invulnerability. Now all humans are forced to live with a keen awareness of how precarious life is. For many this idea of treating our vulnerabilities as intimate companions is so alien we can hardly imagine how to do it. However, right in front of us is a stepping-stone every person can actually use; it is solid and secure and able to hold us firm, even with all our weighty burdens. This book attempts to lay out the emotional treasures that come from living with our vulnerabilities exposed, to both ourselves and to others. And it tries to show the essential character of the journey: learning to walk with the shadows, rather than trying to construct a world where there are no shadows.

I have chosen to write about this theme for several reasons. First, to be fully human today requires a psycho-social-spiritual condition that is hard to even glimpse, but we all need to participate in the discovery and creation of new ways of being. Second, when I was a child my family narrowly escaped from China while the communist revolution of 1949, led by Mao Dedong — one of the most successful terrorists of all time — broke all around us. We adopted the traditional ways of coping. But in my bones, I always knew they were not working. Fleeing did not bring the peace we assumed would come once we were out of the violent environment. To the contrary, what we tried to leave behind traveled with us, was amplified over the decades, and reached an emotional explosiveness far exceeding that which gave it birth. It took me thirty years to begin untangling the emotional, physical, and spiritual knots created by those childhood traumas. Only as I went toward what I wanted to escape did I find relief. Then many surprising and life-sustaining lessons surfaced, ones I imagine will continue to unfold until my final breath. These discoveries that crept up on me seem highly relevant to the shared traumas of this day. Third, I am an organizational psychologist who has spent most of my adult life studying, working within, and writing about human systems in considerable disarray. Over the years my discipline has tapped into some important insights that seem relevant to the journey ahead.

So what lessons are available to those who yearn for a sense of home in these troubled times?

I have chosen to use the ancient art of storytelling, preserved for us by the indigenous peoples of the earth, because stories can access the insights that emerge from the heart more powerfully than logical postulates. No idea that is disconnected from the heart holds any currency for me any longer.

We start by examining the forces that drive people out of their habitats, out of the psychological structures housing their spirits, and lead them to search for new ways to be *at home* in the world.

Instead of looking "out there" for answers, we go to our own backyard; and rather than scrutinize the literally homeless, we focus on the sense of homelessness that resides in each of us.

The first port of call is an educational event called a "Power Laboratory."[1] This is an experiential learning process with a thirty-year tradition. In a Power Lab participants are taken to an isolated setting and upon arrival are randomly assigned to one of three groups: the Elites, the Middles, or the Outs. Each person's birth status determines all the conditions of life for the next several days. The Elites run the mini-society however they choose. The Outs lose all possessions, are given inadequate food, and are allocated poor lodgings. Middles are given satisfactory meals and acceptable accommodation but get caught in the crossfire between the powerful and the powerless. This book tells the stories of two Labs, both structured with the Outs being homeless. In the first one, the Elites and Middles entered into a coalition and tried to save the Outs from their fate. It failed miserably and led to scenes reminiscent of *Animal Farm*. In the second Lab the Elites left the Outs to work out their own destiny, the Middles remained in the middle and mediated the system's conflicts, and the Outs let themselves fall into their homelessness. The results were stunning. The Outs plumbed the depths of their homeless condition, not only at the Lab but in their overall lives, and found a source of power that was transforming.

The middle section of the book chronicles the lessons the participants in the second Lab stumbled upon. They discovered that the inner landscape was a constant enactment of the tensions emerging in the relationship between the *creative self* and the *suffering self*, and moderated by the *accepting self*. Interwoven into the journeys and discoveries of these men and women is an integrative case, my own struggle to find a sense of home, which lasted for decades and required me to return to China and to rest in the bosom of a country that had once tried to kill my family.

The book ends with the realization that to be truly at home, with all the grandeur and mystery that the experience of home evokes, we must collectively and individually discover and rediscover again and again an ancient truth: that, ultimately, home is a condition of the spirit.

# Acknowledgments

This book is an outgrowth of exchanges I had with many students who were deeply curious about why there are so many homeless people in the United States, rejected the superficial explanations, and reflected on a question most people avoid: "In what ways am I too searching for a *sense of home?*" The inquiring spirits of the learners often prompted me to think in new ways, to look at life from a different parapet, and to open my heart to people and themes that make me feel vulnerable. I begin by thanking my students, who courageously asked the unaskable questions, prodded me to think in new ways, and accepted their teacher as a fellow learner. I am very grateful to all who participated in the experiences recorded in this book and then were willing to have their personal stories included. Because of our confidentiality agreement, I cannot name you here, but please know I carry you all in my heart.

I am grateful to all who read drafts of this manuscript and gave me valuable feedback: David Berg, Sara Corse, Dana Kaminstein, Rich Merriman, John Kralovec, Edmund Browning, Corty Cammann, Gene Bay, Annie McKee, Cassie Cammann, Peter Kuriloff, Pattie Kitchen. I also thank my agent, Alice McElhinney, and my publisher, Timothy Staveteig, for their assistance.

Many colleagues served as staff for the Power Labs I have run, often dedicating their services for free. My thanks to each of you: Flora Taylor, Nancie Zane, David Berg, Leroy Wells (deceased), Tom Pitman, Lubin G. Filmartin, Rose Miller, Dahlia Radley, George Brown, Annelise Goldstein, David Thomas, Terry Cumins (deceased), Francisco Moreno, Eduardo Figueroa, Bill Loewen, Cassie Solomon-Giles, Sebastian Demonte, Dana Kaminstein, Clayton Alderfer, James Krantz, Greg Shea, Richard

Hackman, Ana Reyes, Stephanie Boddie. Also thanks to Barry Oshry for creating and refining this educational methodology over the years and for his tutelage half a lifetime ago.

Lastly I thank Sara for the sense of home we have created together, in our West Philadelphia habitat, in our emotional journeying, in our communities near and far, and in our attempts to find a place in this huge mystery called life. Our children, Justin, Phillip, and Kalila, give texture to a life that would have felt bare-boned were it not for the fleshy joys and anguishes they infuse into our days. Kalila, Phillip, Justin, and Sara, this book is as much yours as mine. Thanks for the lessons we have tried to untangle together.

# Chapter 1

# Crying in the Wilderness

## Looking with a Stranger's Eye

It was particularly cold that first winter. I had moved to Philadelphia in the fall, but I already doubted this place would ever
feel like home, this City of Brotherly Love. There was too much
pain. As I walked from work each evening the many images of
humanity's suffering interrupted my private thoughts of a roar-
ing fire and hot chocolate. Every steam vent had been claimed
as a resting place for someone with no home. Drug-dependent
men and women wandered the dark alleyways that by day were
vibrant with industry. The deinstitutionalized declared to anony-
mous passersby their anguished need for mental health care. And
at each corner I was greeted by plaintive eyes and another plea
for my money. It was disquieting. The plight of the homeless,
the drug dependent, the emotionally disturbed made me both
grateful I had a place to go and angry that my journey home
offered no tranquility at day's end. I wanted time to repair, to
restore after my hours of labor. But I did not know how to walk
with my eyes closed. I did not know how to be indifferent to
the plight of others. I did not know how to move between the
worlds of the haves and the have-nots.

Disturbed about feeling disturbed, I decided to volunteer at a
shelter for homeless men in my neighborhood. For months I went
each Thursday night to help serve an evening meal and to be with
these men for a few hours. I was moved by their stories and
always felt a little richer for our time together. I was surprised
by the depth of these men who were slowly but surely inviting
me to open my heart. I did not know how closed I had been.

1

It was clear that each of them was playing a role in a larger sociological drama whose plot neither they nor I could grasp. I was puzzled by how little I understood the forces that made them homeless. The standard explanations about poverty, drug use, unemployment, mental health problems, etc., hardly scratched the surface. I had never taken in who the homeless were, what it was like to be homeless, or the poignant lessons life's struggles had taught them.

On one occasion I was feeling overwhelmed by the events of my life and was telling my shelter buddies about it. Sara, pregnant with our first child, had been the victim of twenty-four-hour-a-day morning sickness for the previous sixteen weeks. We were exhausted and troubled. Then we discovered she was carrying twins. I was delighted but felt overwhelmed by the responsibilities of fathering twins. As I told these men about my anxiety, one beautiful old man, whose wrinkly face comes back to me vividly these many years later, looked me right in the eye and, without missing a beat, said, "The Lord don't ever ask us to do nothin' he ain't prepared us for."

I was calmed by his words. I had heard this message many times before, but it sounded different coming from a homeless man. His exhortation invited me to listen to this expression of comfort in a fresh way. His serenity, his warmth, his tenderness provided the soothing balm my anxious spirit needed. His gift of assurance seemed to come from the Gospel According to the Homeless. "The Lord don't ever ask us to do nothin' he ain't prepared us for." I often wonder about the sense of peace that old African American man exuded. Given the adversities of his life, how had the Lord prepared him? What inner strengths had he been given to cope with the suffering he had been called on to endure?

Working at this shelter led me to revisit something that got my attention when I first came to the United States. I was surprised that a nation with such wealth would have so many homeless people. In the parts of the world I'd visited, homelessness was a result of national poverty or political instability. However, the United States was neither poor nor politically fragile. How could it be that so many people had no place to lay their head? Surely,

I thought, if a nation can send spaceships to dance with the stars and stockpile arsenals to destroy the world many times over, it could end homelessness if it were a national priority.

I deliberated at length about what made it so hard for such a wealthy nation to mobilize the political will needed to solve this social plight. None of the standard explanations seemed to go beneath the surface. So I began asking the question in a different way. If the nation's body politic perpetuates homelessness, albeit unwittingly, could it be that the homeless fulfill a function for the society as a whole? And if so, what function might that be?

During my search to understand homelessness, I came across a few lines from Jelaluddin Rumi, the thirteenth-century mystic poet from the region now known as Afghanistan and Turkey, that crystallized this dilemma eloquently:

> No matter how fast you run,
> Your shadow more than keeps up.
> Sometimes, it's in front!
>
> Only full, overhead sun
> diminishes your shadow.
>
> But that shadow has been serving you!
> What hurts you, blesses you.
> Darkness is your candle.[2]

Emboldened by this ancient sage I reformulated my question and asked, "How does homelessness serve us?" Is it the shadow that shows us we cannot run away? Is it the darkness that reminds us of the light? As I thought about what the homeless might be expressing for us all, some new images emerged. When I saw people who were worse off than I was, I felt thankful for what I had. Also the homeless reminded me about the fragility of the sociopolitical structures upon which my well-being rested. "There but for the grace of God go I" was a refrain that came easily when I took in their predicament.

Another image was more metaphoric. Just as the light and dark co-define each other, the lives of the homeless showed me the ways I have a home. As I saw those with no place to call their own, no place to rest, no place that offered a safe haven, I was grateful for my possessions, for the safety I felt as I locked my door each night, for restful sleep. However, a closer look revealed another side to this reality: my possessions often owned me; the hours between midnight and dawn were but a brief pause in the endless barrage of work, family, and community demands; the bars on our windows, the screeching sirens of the night, and the polluted breezes that infused our bedrooms on a hot summer's night all pointed to the ways contemporary life threatened us. None of this took away from the value of the things we had, of nocturnal respite, of the security we enjoyed, but it showed me that the anguish of the homeless was my anguish as well. There were many ways in which I did not feel at home in this world even though I owned a physical habitat.

My musing launched me on a search to find the ways in which I did not feel at home. That quest took me to some faraway places and challenged me to find the familiar in the unfamiliar. It provoked me to visit some spots so close I had never noticed them, and challenged me to find the unfamiliar in the familiar. This proved to be the most significant journey I had ever undertaken. I discovered that in the hidden crevices of my spirit I had been searching for a way to be at home in this world for a very long time and for reasons I had never understood. In my case, primal fear had held me captive since childhood and it was hard to grasp why or how it had been shaping my essence. Much later I was to learn that the essence of my own story and of every person I know is the struggle to find a way to be at home in a world growing increasingly fragmented.

## What Is Home?

To understand why someone might be literally homeless or feel "not at home," we need to grasp what is meant by "home." At the basic level home is a physical location: it is where we sleep at night, the place where we store our treasures and the necessities required for daily living, the spot that serves as our point of reference, the center from which we leave and to which we return when we are done, the haven where we can relax and be ourselves without fear of consequences. Every person needs a home in this sense. So when we speak of home we refer, at the very least, to this *physical* reality.

However, home is much more than this. It is also a metaphor that represents something deeper, broader, and loftier.

In the deeper sense, we speak of feeling "at home" within ourselves. This is addressing a psychological sense of home. It symbolizes a level of internal integration where the discordant and contradictory impulses of our humanity are at peace and we are able to be in a state of calm in our relationships with others. When we are "at home" with ourselves we feel our inner core is intact and we know what is central and what is peripheral for us. We refer to this as our *emotional* home.

In the broader sense, we speak of feeling "at home" in our community. This represents a sociological sense of home. It signifies belonging to a network of interdependent relationships where people know our names, where we are comfortable telling our stories, where we look out for one another, where we feel nourished by the giving of ourselves, and where the common good is important for our individual well-being. This is our *communal* home.

In the loftier sense, we speak of feeling "at home" in our relationship with Yahweh, Tao, the Great Spirit, God. This epitomizes a spiritual sense of home. It denotes our relationship with the transcendent, with the eternal, with the mystery of life itself. We think of this as our *sacred* home.

To feel "at home" requires all four of these, the physical, the emotional, the communal, and the sacred. The definition of home offered by Henri Nouwen draws together all four of these dimensions: "Home is that place or space where we do not have to be afraid, but can let go of our defenses and be free, free from worries, free from tensions, free from pressures. Home is where we can laugh and cry, embrace and dance, sleep long and dream quietly, eat, read, play, watch the fire, listen to music, and be with a friend. Home is where we can rest and be healed.... [It is] the house of love."[3]

"Home" and "homeless" are concepts that co-define each other. To fully understand home requires an appreciation of the ways we are served by our homelessness and vice versa. There are numerous examples of the way growth results from losing our home.

At the individual level, the early steps toward independence and, ultimately, interdependence are taken when we leave the family home and set off to be on our own. This is an unsettling time, but for most the instability is useful. Leaving the comforts of the familiar, and the precariousness that attends such departures, prepares us to make a home in some other place.

Another example is the artist who refuses to operate within the accepted conventions of the day. There is agony for those who push the boundaries of our consciousness. They face rejection at every turn and yet courageously continue to express what their hearts decree. Each knows that the more creative the work, the greater the probability it will be shunned in the artistic world, at least initially. Creativity might lead to acceptance someday, but it will probably first produce artistic homelessness. Later we may take those composers of the new into our hearts and witness the shattering of the limits once used to reject them. Then we see that their tenacious carrying on in the face of artistic rejection was what gave birth to a community of acceptance for those who came after them.

Throughout history a scourge of so-called civilization has been the homelessness inflicted on those placed into slavery. We have seen this with the Jews of old in Egypt, the five million Manchurians captured to build the Great Wall of China, and the countless millions of Africans upon whose backs the colonialists and the imperialists built their new world order. These peoples, forced to endure generations of homelessness, had no option but to seek a sense of home in some place other than the physical.

Despite the horror that has attended the homeless through the ages, we recognize that this darkness has proved to be humanity's light. Many of the spiritual lessons of history have been learned on pilgrimage, while living in exile, during periods of incarceration, and in the face of a community's scorn and rejection. It has often been through the loss of our homes that we have learned about the essence of our spirituality. This has been such a prevalent motif for capturing the sacred that the journey through life itself is often described as "going home" and death as a final "homecoming."[4]

## Are We All Homeless?

Humanity's ageless search for home is an acknowledgment of the universal character of homelessness. This is not merely an affliction that strikes those unable to find a safe place to sleep but is something located in the core of each person. When we see it solely as a characteristic of those who occupy our city vents and ask for our change in the subway, we fail to recognize that they are enacting something on our collective behalf. We are all striving to be at home with our conflicting emotions. We are all struggling to remain integrated in the face of societal pressures tearing our lives apart. We are all trying to find a way into the inner sanctuary of our beings.[5]

The search to find a way to be at home in the world is something all humanity has in common. This is not a characteristic only of those who live on the streets. That is just a visible form of something most of us keep hidden. While some live out our yearning for home in a highly visible way, the rest of us keep it masked. Could it be that the homeless express something on behalf of us all so we don't have to feel it so keenly ourselves? Could it be that we collectively create homelessness as a way to hide from some painful truths about our shared nature? Could it be that this social dis-ease is an invitation to accept some truths we wish to ignore? Could it be that the inner sense of homelessness from which we hide is so central to the human condition that if it were not expressed in its present form, it would come out in some other way?

Everyone feels homeless at some point in life. When we are ill, when foreign germs make us alien to ourselves, it is hard to feel at home in our bodies. When a loved one dies, it is tough to feel at home in the normal routine of our lives. When a community is in crisis, we must be out on the streets helping the wounded, crushed, and bereaved to feel at home with ourselves. When we embrace the feelings of homelessness that we all experience in some part of our beings, we develop the capacity to make enemies into allies and discover that the healing we crave is held in the firm hands of those we live in opposition with. I do not mean just the enemies overseas, but the ones that we harbor inside ourselves and that we work hard not to recognize as we look into the mirror.

Ironic though this may sound, perhaps today's misfits, especially those who want the current systems torn down, are trying to teach us about the real meaning of home. Maybe the homeless, the naysayers, those who live outside society's conventions, are crying in the wilderness and suggesting that we must all find a new way to be in the world.

As we enter the vexing question about how to feel at home in this troubled world, there are warnings that the path is not easy. An ancient Egyptian prayer discovered in the tomb of King Tutankhamen signaled this clearly: "God be between you and harm, in the empty places you must walk." The sages of long ago knew that we had to "walk into the empty places, into the void, into the shadows," for only by going through the barren terrain, the wilderness, can we find a way to be at home in our emotional, our communal, and our sacred selves.

> *Out of my depths have I cried out...*
> *let your ears be attentive to my pleas.*
> Psalm 130:1–2

# Chapter 2

# Violence Is the Language of the Unheard

## Reality TV

A recent trend in the entertainment industry is a phenomenon referred to as "Reality TV." The best-known shows are *Survivor* and *Big Brother*, in which people are put in unfamiliar settings or asked to do unorthodox things while their every move is filmed. These simulations produce moments of high drama embedded in many hours of tedious, everyday processes. What is aired is designed to entertain. While these programs could provide valuable learning, their educational potential has yet to be tapped, and to date the dynamics have been kept at a rather superficial level. Other shows, like *The 1940s House* and *The Trench*, made for British TV, and the PBS series *Frontier House*, illustrate a facet of human history. *The Trench* films people struggling with the daily grind of life in a dugout similar to those that World War I troops experienced. The other two programs show, respectively, a modern family operating in a house equipped as in wartime Britain, with food and luxury items rationed at World War II levels, and three contemporary families facing the Montana wilderness of the 1880s.

This form of entertainment has its roots in simulations designed for educational purposes. Best known are the flight simulators used for pilot training, war games designed to train the

---

This chapter was first published under the same title in the *Journal of Applied Behavioral Science* 38, no. 1 (2002): 6–16; reprinted here with permission. The phrase in the title of this chapter was used often by Martin Luther King Jr. in his speeches.

military, and negotiation workshops to teach about international relations or the making of business deals.[6]

## Learning about Power Relationships

One well-established genre of simulated learning is called the Power Laboratory. As mentioned briefly in the preface, in a typical Lab a number of participants are taken to an isolated setting and upon arrival are randomly assigned to one of three groups: the Elites, the Middles, or the Outs.[7] The Elites are invited to design and run the mini-society however they choose. In return they are given excellent food, luxurious accommodations, and control over discretionary resources. The Outs have very little. Middles get adequate food and good living quarters, but are beholden to the Elites and feel the heat of the Outs' rage over anything that goes wrong.

People sign on for these programs because they want visceral learning to augment their academic understanding about the dynamics of power, powerlessness, and being caught in the middle. Sometimes a Power Lab ends up like *Lord of the Flies*. Other times it plays out in a way that is highly productive and stirs optimism in the human heart. No matter how it unfolds the participants make profound discoveries about group dynamics, organizational and societal politics, and the possibilities of personal and systemic transformation.

Several faculty serve as "anthropologists" during the simulated community experience and silently observe as much of the action as possible. The deep learning occurs during a two-day review of the whole process conducted by the faculty immediately after the experiential component of the Lab.

When Power Labs are described, a common reaction is that the participants were just role-playing. However, the group dynamics become serious very quickly and the intensity of the interactions far exceeds what is seen on a so-called reality TV show. I have run Labs for over two decades, but I am still surprised by the speed with which each group gets entangled in the power dynamics that are linked to its birth status. And participants consistently report that they see great similarity between how they behaved and how workers, bosses, and supervisors function in everyday settings.

Once the original structures of the Power Laboratory are in place and the Elites and Middles are inducted into their respective groups, all decisions are exclusively in the hands of the participants. There is no script to follow: no one instructs them about what to do, advises them about what to avoid, or informs them about what the other groups are scheming.

Beforehand, all applicants are fully briefed about what they are getting into and are screened to ensure that the psychologically precarious and those undergoing extreme stress do not enroll. Participants sign appropriate waivers, including an explicit agreement to be held accountable to the laws of the country and the state in which the Power Lab is being run.

Once, while preparing to teach a class for graduate students at the University of Pennsylvania, I was contemplating whether to include a Power Laboratory as part of the experience, as I sometimes do. Twenty-five students from several of our graduate schools (Wharton, Social Work, Education, Nursing, Communication) had enrolled and expressed their interest in a Lab. I agreed to conduct one. This is their story.[8]

## Beginning the Journey

I decided to run a homeless Lab, which meant there would be no food or accommodations provided for the Outs. So I rented a facility with two buildings at Beacon Hill outside Philadelphia: the Manor House for the seven Elites and the Village Inn for the nine Middles. The Manor was a gorgeous mansion standing alone on a hill, with private bedrooms and bathrooms for each Elite, catered meals, and full cleaning services for their bedrooms. One hundred and fifty yards away, down a winding lane through some leafy woods and across a road, was the Village Inn. In every bedroom at the Inn there were four beds, but only two people were assigned to each room. No meals were provided for the Middles, but the Inn had a well-equipped, institutional kitchen. The Elites were given enough money to buy high-quality produce for the Middles, who could cook for themselves and be well sustained.

At the Inn and the Manor there were enough spare beds for the eleven Outs if the participants chose to reorganize their society. Also, if the Elites lowered the quality of Middle meals to summer camp level, there was sufficient money for the Outs to be adequately fed as well.

The Elites and Middles were inducted into this mini-society and transported to Beacon Hill on a Tuesday night. The Elites were given all the resources and were told that the Outs were destined to arrive about noon the next day.

The Elites asked the Middles to help design the mini-society. For many hours, they wrestled with what to do about the Outs and ultimately decided to construct a "nonhomeless" society. They rearranged the living conditions so there was a bed for every Out and purchased enough food for everyone to be adequately fed. By the time the Outs arrived, all vestiges of homelessness would have been eliminated. At least that was the plan.

## Eat Now, This Might Be Your Last Meal

One thing that was unusual about the Beacon Hill experience was that all participants knew one another. They had all spent a semester together in class and were eagerly anticipating the Lab. They expected the conditions to be extreme and for days had been readying themselves.

Although the Outs were not being registered for the Lab until Wednesday morning, by 9:00 p.m. Tuesday they learned that some people had already departed for Beacon Hill. So the individuals who were left behind started calling each other to figure out who was still around. By 11:00 p.m. they had worked out that there were eleven of them who had not yet gone. They correctly deduced they were to be the Outs. Knowing they would probably be underfed over the next few days, all of them began a greedy eating process lasting for hours. Most of them sat up all night gorging themselves. Although they were right that they were to be the Outs, they had no clue that they were destined to be homeless. By the following morning, they had eaten so much there was no possibility any of them was remotely hungry. Nevertheless, as they came to campus at 8:00 a.m. to register, many were still shoving pastry and fruit into their mouths.

The "birthing" ritual for the Outs was severe. They had to hand over all their possessions — car keys, money, credit cards, IDs, bags, and so on — keeping only the clothes on their backs. They all complied, while both protesting and engaging in humorous banter. The Outs knew that surrendering their possessions meant they would have few material resources until after the Lab. Once all the Outs had registered they were each given a dollar and told: "Please do not spend this; you will need it for tomorrow; *if* you eat and *what* you eat will depend on your having this dollar bill." Apart from that, the Outs were told nothing about where they were going or what awaited them. They were asked to follow the registrar, who then walked them the eight city blocks to Philadelphia's main railway station at 30th Street. During this hike to the station, they were on familiar territory. These were streets they walked every day, yet these Outs acted like terrified adolescents. They moved as if tied to each other by an invisible string. No one was ever more than a few feet away from another member of the group.

By the time they reached the station, every one of them had spent his or her dollar. They had not gone a block before someone complained of being hungry. Once one wanted food, all did. They stopped at the various street vendors on the way to the station and bought pretzels, muffins, and junk food. They all seemed genuinely starving. Yet it was not even ten o'clock and only an hour or two since they had finished probably the largest eating binge of their lives. There was no way that their bodies lacked food. Their desire to eat had to come from a cavernous place within them other than their stomachs. There was a strong group component to this hunger as well. At no stage did anyone say, "Remember we were told this dollar was going to be critical to our survival later on." The banter was "This is survival time! Eat now, for there may not be a tomorrow! Ain't no use having cash and not spend'n it when you need it!" As these participants squandered the only money they would see for days, it was obvious they had left the realm of conventional rationality and were being driven by forces out of their awareness.

## The Homeless of 30th Street Station

By the time the Outs arrived at 30th Street Station, there was no doubt they were a group. Upon discovering that all their dollars were gone, they were undisturbed. They congratulated themselves on having the foresight not to take the money with them. "That would just give *them* one more thing to take away from *us,*" was their conclusion.

"What will we do if they give us no food?" asked one.

"No problem!" came a chorus of voices.

With that, four of them took off to search for discarded food. They rummaged through the trash cans at the station, stuffing half-eaten McDonald's hamburgers and leftover bread rolls into their pockets. From the outside, their behavior looked pitiful. However, when the scavengers came to tell their fellow Outs about how much food they had gathered, their success was greeted with cheers. All were proud of their accomplishments.

After a twenty-minute wait, the registrar gave each of them a ticket, escorted them to a platform, and said, "Please get on this train pulling in right now and get off at Millers' Glen. Someone will be there to direct you to where the Lab is being held." The Outs' reaction to being told to get on the train was to huddle and ask if this was wise. By the time they had all expressed their views the train had long since gone. "No problem," said one of them. "Why bother going there to be an Out when you we can be an Out here. At least we've got a roof over our head!" "And food in our pockets," added another as he patted the stale hamburger meat in his pocket. Their view was "what's the point of rushing to an unknown *there* which promises nothing more than *here?*" Over the next hour, the Outs made quite a nuisance of themselves at 30th Street Station. They were unschooled in the art of being Outs in public places, and the police would not let them take a nap on the benches or to congregate in the rest rooms, because they were too bawdy and raucous. The rebellious spirits of these Outs had been activated, and they no longer respected the social conventions that sustain civility. Although they were graduate students at a prestigious university, those waiting to board a train for Washington or New York saw them as Philadelphia's real down and outs. They were already acting like the homeless even though they still had no idea this was the status slated for them at Beacon Hill, a place they did not know even existed.

In time, the Outs got bored and decided to leave. Someone remembered that the train they had not caught had left at 10:39. "I'll bet the one leaving from the same platform at 11.39 will go to Millers' Glen," suggested one of them. So they huddled on the platform, letting train after train go by, and then, when one pulled in at 11:39, they jumped aboard. They seemed not to realize that these trains could be off schedule, nor did they ask the staff if the train they were boarding was going to Millers' Glen.

By sheer luck, the Outs got on the right train. Then, for the next half hour, every time it stopped, they peered out the window to see if they were at the station they wanted. Again it did not occur to them to ask the conductor how many stops it was to Millers' Glen or to check the map on the train. During their journey, they formulated and chanted what has become known as the Outs' credo:

> Do not trust them, for whoever they are, they will try to manipulate us; stick together because we have strength in numbers; our unity will make us more powerful than the other groups; before any Out takes an individual action, first get approval from the whole group; a resource one gets is a resource for the whole group and is to be shared with all the Outs.

By the time they arrived at Millers' Glen, the Outs had dreamed of everything that could possibly happen. No matter what they confronted, their strategy was the same: Stick together! Don't let them drive a wedge between us and make us weak. Refuse to become their pawns. Whatever they want, we want the opposite.

Despite the fact the Outs were an hour later than anticipated, two members of the Beacon Hill society were at the station when they disembarked. This first moment of encounter was very intense and presaged what the next few days were to be like.

## We Oppose Everything You Favor

The Elites were proud of having redesigned Beacon Hill so that no one would be homeless. They believed that by rearranging the sleeping quarters and purchasing food for all, the homeless problem was solved. They assumed the Outs would despise their Outness and would take any opportunity to become more like the Middles or the Elites. They never dreamed that the Outs might be nourished by their feelings of contempt for the world they had been born into or that they might detest those who used material privileges to define their status. The Elites and Middles were convinced that the new arrivals would be grateful for having been saved from their destiny. Hence, they were unprepared for how the Outs reacted.

The "redesigned society," as the former Elites and Middles called Beacon Hill, had carefully chosen one Elite and one Middle, Joan and Jonathan, to go to Millers' Glen to welcome the Outs. Having a person from each group was meant to communicate that the Elites and Middles were unified, a symbol that eluded the Outs, for they did not know who belonged to any group other than their own or what the group distinctions meant. The special appeal of Joan and Jonathan was that they had good relationships with everyone during earlier class interactions. Care had been taken not to send any of the abrasive characters from the Elite-Middle ranks who might trigger unwanted reactions in the Outs.

The scene at Millers' Glen had the flavor of a rural political rally, minus the high school band. The speeches had been carefully crafted, and the audience was expected to applaud politely and go along with the script. Joan was designated as the first to welcome the Outs as they alighted from the train. She started innocently. "On behalf of all the members of Beacon Hill already assembled, I would like to welcome you."

"Who are *you?*" came a quick Out retort, dripping with sarcasm.

"I am a member of the welcoming committee," replied Joan calmly. "I have come here to accompany you to our society."

"*What* society!"

"Beacon Hill."

"What's Beacon Hill?"

"Follow me, and I will take you there," Joan said.

"We are not following anyone anywhere!" came a chorus of Out voices.

The noisy hostility coming from the Outs silenced Joan. She was genuinely puzzled as to why they were reacting this way. She expected that welcoming the Outs would be easy. She never imagined they might view her as an enemy or that those who had been her friends last week would now make her the target of their anger. The Outs seemed rage-filled, but Joan could not do anything about it. She was also feeling hurt. The Elites and Middles had labored hard to improve the Outs' lot, hoping that everyone would have a pleasant time at Beacon Hill. Yet the Outs were being belligerent, even though no one had done a thing to them.

Jonathan jumped in, trying to support Joan. Shouting him down, the Outs wouldn't even let him speak. The more kindly Joan and Jonathan tried to be, the angrier the Outs became. They refused to listen to anything. After a while, the Outs huddled, as if to strategize about what actions to take next. They appeared to be caucusing to plan their next move, but they did nothing more than congratulate themselves on how effectively they were opposing Joan and Jonathan.

Joan tried again. "All I wanted to do was show you how to get to Beacon Hill. It's about a half-mile walk."

"We're not following you anywhere, any time. Don't you get it!" replied an angry Out. The Outs had defined Joan as an enemy not because of what she'd done but because she was not one of them. After several more frustrating attempts to engage these angry newcomers, Joan and Jonathan decided it was futile. So they left. As they disappeared around a curve in the road, it dawned on the Outs that they could now be stranded. They had no money, no train tickets, and no knowledge of where they were. This promised to be a dilemma.

Quickly resolving to follow Joan and Jonathan from a distance, they broke into a sprint in a frantic attempt to catch up. However, they did not want to be seen, so once they had the escorts in sight, the Outs skirted furtively from tree to tree, hoping to learn about Beacon Hill without being discovered. Here they were, following the very people they had decided not to, yet they were doing it in a way that helped them preserve the illusion that they did not have to depend on anyone and that their destiny was exclusively in their own hands.

## We've Found the Food Supply

Once they got to Beacon Hill, the Outs hid behind some shrubbery atop a grassy knoll overlooking the retreat center. For a while, they watched the interactions among the Elite-Middles, who did not realize that the Outs had arrived at Beacon Hill and were spying on them. The Elites were distressed that their attempts to improve things for the have-nots had been rebuffed. Of course, the Outs still did not know that they had originally been designated the homeless or that the whole mini-society had been redesigned to make them not homeless.

At this point, the haves were at a loss about what to do. The only reason for their existence had been to save the have-nots from homelessness. What does a system do when its purpose is to save the homeless from their fate and the homeless don't show up? The irony did not elude the powerful, who recognized that they depended on the assumed neediness of the Outs for a cause to unite them. They felt paralyzed by the Outs' refusal to fit into the category slotted for them. Their fantasy was that the Outs would be grateful to be given food and a bed and would want to join in the formation of an egalitarian society. Yet the Outs had rejected the Beacon Hill society even before encountering it.

As the Outs watched from their hilltop perch, they deduced that there were two houses, one that was open to all and another accessible to only a select few. They accurately concluded that the mansion was the Elites' home and the other was for the Middles. When it was clear no one was around, three scouts were sent to check out the Manor. They were instructed to keep their presence clandestine.

The scouts crawled commando-style from bush to bush, successfully avoiding being seen. However, the stealth they used to get to the Manor had put them into the mind-set of burglars. Upon starting out, it was not clear what they would do when they arrived at the Manor. Once there, however, the only obvious thing to do was to check if the house was locked. It was. So the next self-evident thing to do was to break in. To get in on the ground floor would have required breaking some glass; however, a window over the porch on the second floor gave way easily. Within seconds, the three were standing inside the Elite house. They gave each other high fives, while the other Outs, watching the break-in from their perch on the hill, let out a muffled cheer.

Once inside, what were they going to do? Obviously, check things out! The scouts went into the first bedroom and started rifling though the drawers. "I wonder who is sleeping here?" one asked as he emptied a drawer and threw clothes all over the floor. "Oh, I recognize this sweater. This is John. So John's an Elite! He'll be tough to deal with."

On to the next room. It was clearly occupied by a woman. "Ah, here are some birth control pills. This is sure to be Joan," was the conclusion they reached as they dumped her bras and panties in a pile on the floor.

The scouts went through every room trying to decipher who belonged to the Elites, leaving the house thoroughly trashed.

They then stumbled on the food that had been purchased for Middle and Out meals. The trio did not know what this food was for, since they had not yet learned of the mini-society's design or the fact they had been slated to be homeless. However, they found comfort in knowing where food was stored and that they could break in at any time and steal it. Upon leaving the Manor, the scouts rigged a basement window so it could not be locked again, creating an easy access to the food supply. "There is no reason why any Out should go hungry again," they said as they helped themselves to two bags of cookies, which they took back to their comrades still hiding behind the bushes overlooking Beacon Hill.

When the burglars rejoined the Outs, they celebrated together the success of this mission by ceremoniously eating the stolen cookies.

In time, the Outs were seen by the other members of Beacon Hill and started engaging with them. That was when they learned, for the first time, that they were to be homeless and had been saved from this fate by the unilateral decisions of the Elites and the Middles.

## How Dare You Tell Us Who We Are!

To cut a very long story short, the Outs of Beacon Hill refused ever to sleep in a bed. By night, they huddled on the floor of the Village Inn, using shared body heat as their way of keeping warm. However, they did eat. After all, this was a group that was perpetually hungry! They agreed to be the cooks for the Middles, and their reward was to be able to eat too. They were satisfied that this was not a form of charity, and construed it as their job. Beyond that, they refused ever to cooperate with the Elites or the Middles.

In addition, after every meal when no Elite was around, the Outs broke into the Manor and stole some more food.

Eventually, they were caught stealing. The Elites responded by threatening to cut off all food if the stealing did not stop. This fueled more thieving and put the Elites into a worse quandary: continue being benevolent and be exploited, or stop all generosity and become like the depriving Elites they never wanted to be? The Elites made the Manor into a fortress. The result? The Outs used even more force to break in.

At one point, there was a great face-to-face showdown. The Elites and Middles were flabbergasted that these former friends and classmates had become thieves and with genuine anger asked, "What made you Outs into thieves and robbers? We have treated you well and have been willing to give you everything we had. Yet you keep stealing from us. Don't you get it? From the beginning, our position has been that you could just ask us for whatever you need and we'd give it to you. Why did you insist on stealing from us? What made you so violent? What turned you into a den of thieves?"

The response was spine-chilling and is one of the great moments in Power Lab history.

## We Were Born Homeless and We Will Die Homeless!

"Don't you dare call us thieves!" yelled the Outs back at them as the conflict escalated.

"Why? That's what you are! Violent thugs, who will steal from the very people who are providing for you everything you have!"

"We're not the thieves here," came the stormy reply from the Outs. "You are!" The Elites and Middles were stunned by this accusation and the vehemence with which it was delivered. They had no idea what the Outs were saying.

"What are you talking about?" the Elites exclaimed. "Every day you steal food from us! What did we ever do to you? We were never violent toward you. We never stole a single thing from you."

"Take a look at yourselves, you bunch of thieves," said an angry Out. "We are not the violent ones here. You are! We just reflect your violence."

"You're crazy!" said an Elite, getting more furious.

The Outs continued. "Get honest with yourselves. We had one and only one thing: our identity as the homeless! And you felt free to rip that away from us. Without any consultation! And why did you do this? Because it would be good for us? No! So you would not have to live with the feelings of running a system where we were free to be what we really are, the homeless! You claimed you made these changes to help us. What a lie! You did it to alleviate your own feelings. And don't tell us that is not violence. Ripping the soul out of a people is as violent as it gets."

The Elites and Middles were stunned.

"It is true," said an Out, "that we took cookies from your home. But that is minuscule in contrast to what you stole from us. We are not thieves! You just see in our behavior something that is true about you, but you will not admit it. What is the greater sin? Our stealing your cookies? Or your stealing our birthright?"

This was a truly sobering moment for those who had dedicated their lives to saving the homeless of Beacon Hill.

Defensively an Elite asked, "But why did you keep breaking in and taking more food? You couldn't have been hungry, and if you were, we'd have given you more food?"

Back came a startling response. "And that's where the problem lies. The have-nots have to keep stealing so that we don't ever lose the art form. Because we never know when you haves will cut off the food supply. We figure you will do it immediately after we've forgotten how to be effective thieves. So we steal to keep our survival crafts alive. We know what we are doing and why. But what about you? Why do you go around stealing the emotions, destiny, and dignity of others? Do you know why you do this? Or do you just do this because it's what you do and you have no clue what you are up to?"

The Elites and Middles of Beacon Hill seemed unable to come up with any response, so an Out continued. "You Elites did not make us homeless in the first place, but you presumed to take our birthright from us. Who do you think you are? You are trying to play God! If God made us this way, only God can take it away! If you try to alter who we are, then you are acting as if you are God yourselves. Don't you understand that! Don't you see that our pain, our deprivation, is the only thing we have? It is the basis of all the horrible feelings we have toward the world. Take that away and we are left with all these awful feelings with no place to dump them. To take that away from us is like ripping out our soul! We don't have much but we do have our identity and our dignity. We might want to free ourselves from homelessness, but we don't want you taking it from us!"

## The Death of Some Old Thoughts

When the hostility calmed down and the Elites were willing to hear what the Outs were saying, this was what they heard: "You

Elites don't seem to recognize that you seized the power latent in your position and, not liking the social arrangements you inherited, preceded to reinvent society to fit your own aspirations. You wanted Beacon Hill to be free of social problems. But you focused on things like beds and food. You seemed to define all relationships in terms of what things you or we had or lacked. Since we did not have any things, what was important to us was different. All we had was problems and our responses to those problems. How we reacted to the struggles we confronted was what gave our Out group its life. The more things you wanted to give us, the more our way of life was threatened and the more beholden we knew we would be to you. Even though we might have wanted the material benefits you had, a much bigger motivation for us was to never become like you. To accept your way of life would be equivalent to killing ourselves. We also knew that stealing your cookies would drive you nuts. We didn't want or need your cookies. But showing you that you were powerless to stop us was very satisfying. The more you lorded over us the fact you had the food to give us, the more we wanted to drive you crazy. So we looked for something simple to get at you. It worked. We forced you to become the people you never wanted to be, mean and defensive. And of course, you did not know how to cope as mean and defensive people. But we did. We lowered you to our level and we felt proud that we had shifted you off your pedestal."

As things became calmer the Middle group grew distressed that they were seen as fused with the Elites. This was what the Outs got across to them: "When you Middles joined the Elites, you lost your utility to the whole system. You Elites-Middles, you haves, were a formidable coalition. When we Outs dug in our heels and refused to go along with your wishes, the system became intensely polarized and there was no middle group to act as a buffer between the extreme positions or to mediate the tensions that arose from those extremes. Look at it. The Elites have the power to construct. The Outs have the power to reject. The Middles have the power to mediate. What happens when the Outs reject what the Elites construct? If the Middles throw their lot in with the Elites, there is no mediating force available in the system. It is equally problematic when Middles align with the Outs in rejecting what the Elites are constructing. In each case the situation grows more polarized and it is hard to keep relationships from spiraling into a disintegrated state. Every human system requires integration, but this demands that some people take on the middle function."

The Outs concluded, Had we been Beacon Hill's homeless, we would have felt like pawns in the hands of history with no place to dump our anger. But to be the nonhomeless would have made us puppets in your hands. It was satisfying to have real people we could get angry at. That was how you played into our hands. Your actions made it easy for us to be furious at you.

## *Another Perspective*

During the review period it was clear that once the Outs moved to their rebellious and rejecting posture, the Elites became hurt. Had they set out to be unkind, the Outs' reaction might have felt understandable. However, since they thought they were doing the right thing, they saw this rejection as a repudiation of them as people. Given the Elites' blind spots, their question was "Why are the Outs treating us this way?" not "What message are they conveying to us, the people responsible for Beacon Hill?" Having formulated the issue in personalized terms, the only answer they were able to construct was "because they are irresponsible types with destructive tendencies!"

That way of construing the situation set in place a range of problematic attributions. Question: "Why won't they sleep in the beds we provided them?" Answer: "Because they are losers!" Alternative interpretation not considered: "They want to preserve their sense of unity; being our guests and sleeping in our bedrooms will fragment them and undermine their sense of togetherness." Question: "Why do they steal from us the food we are willing to give them?" Answer: "Because they are a bunch of criminals!" Alternative interpretation not considered: "Their stealing tells us they do not accept our authority; receiving the food as charity reinforces our authority and makes them feel that they are not able to care for themselves."

The Elite-Middle coalition did not recognize that the Outs' actions were an attempt to communicate. Instead of viewing this as a message, the Elites interpreted it as an act of aggression, which led them to behave in dictatorial and retaliatory ways, the antithesis of how they had set out to be. On the other side of the equation, the Outs were angry and had only one way to express this: "Whatever you want we oppose because you want it." They were not able to define themselves on their own terms. Instead they merely reacted to how others treated them. In many ways the character of the haves was a product of how the have-nots reacted to them and vice versa.

There was tremendous communal angst as the Beacon Hill society ached and groaned its way into existence. In the interactions among these three groups, two forces were pitted in opposition to each other. The energies to construct a desirable world were at war with the energies invested in destroying the world as it is. Since there was no mechanism to mediate these polarities or to draw them into complementary parts of a larger whole, nothing worth preserving emerged from these opposing forces. It did not have to be this way, however.

The twin forces of *construction* and *destruction* are each other's opposite and each other's complement. Neither is possible without the other. At a conceptual level one cannot construct something new without accessing the forces of destruction; at the very least, the new destroys what was there prior to its arrival; otherwise it would not have been interpreted as new.[9]

The Elites and Middles started their lives at Beacon Hill by trying to destroy the social order they inherited. They wanted to use the Outs as an instrument of that destruction by having them be something the Elite-Middle coalition defined. The Outs, in turn, wanted to destroy what this coalition was trying to construct so they could create their own experience. However, trying to make each party into something it was not meant all groups were shaped by destructive energies, even though both the haves and the have-nots construed their own actions in constructive terms.

Every human system requires the juxtaposition of creation and destruction to be alive. Every inhaled breath relies on the exhaling of the one before and the one after. All the new cells that are forming in each person's body depend on the expulsion and destruction of the previous cells. To fully be in this moment means that the last moment has passed away. To make things even more difficult, part of the creative possibility of this moment is based on the reality that it too shall be destroyed by whatever comes after it.

For something meaningful to emerge from the interchange of the constructive and destructive, however, they must be connected. They must be drawn together and allowed to be complementary parts of a whole. That is where the role of middleness is critical. This function of drawing together, of integrating the polarities, is also crucial. It was what Beacon Hill lacked most. It was the role that the Middles left empty when they sided with the Elites.

All human systems are driven by three powerful energies: construction, destruction, and integration function like the three legs of a tripod. They provide the foundation upon which the life of a vital human system rests.

*Deal kindly with us, O Lord....*
*Too long have we had to suffer the insults of the wealthy.*

Psalm 123:3–4

# Chapter 3

# Enriched by Poverty

## Doubting Certainty

In many Power Labs the Elites and Middles have restructured their mini-society in the hope of producing an egalitarian system.[10] These participants are certain that giving everyone the same resources will bring calm. It never works because those in power fail to realize the many ways equality can be understood: Elites think of it in material terms and assume that once food and housing are similar, all will be well; Middles view it as a feature of governance and want everyone involved in decision making; the Outs, while liking the benefits, see it as a ploy to co-opt them, reduce their rage, and undermine their solidarity. When groups try to create an egalitarian system, the Elites focus on redistributing resources, the Middles work to build decision-making processes all will accept, and the Outs seek reparations for the historical wrongs done to them. If these three orientations were seen as complementary, the outcome might be different, but usually they are pitted in opposition to each other and the groups become like ships passing in the night.

A few years after Beacon Hill, I ran another homeless Lab at Fellowship Farm. It produced patterns never previously seen. The structure was similar to Beacon Hill, but the processes were very different; what transpired was so transformative and uplifting I was awestruck.

What was the difference that made it unique?

The Farm Elites accepted that the Outs were homeless and provided for them, but treated them as a group with interests of its own and got on with the task of running the mini-society as best they could. The Middles maintained their middle position

27

and did not move into a coalition with the Elites or the Outs. Hence the Farm had a group both buffering and mediating the natural hostilities that emerged from the opposing interests of the Elites and the Outs.

Like the have-nots of Beacon Hill, the Farm Outs decided to remain homeless, but they reveled in the riches associated with having nothing, blamed no one for their fate, and chose to be fully who they were. Although lacking physical possessions, they treated their world as filled with abundance, doubted the veracity of conventional wisdom, and saw their neediness as a treasure and not as a problem to be solved. Instead of demanding that others take care of them, they elected to nourish each other emotionally. In the process these Outs discovered the key to one of the great, ageless mysteries: when we give of ourselves to one another there is more than enough to go around, but when we try to get as much as we can for ourselves there is never enough for anyone.

The Farm participants were students from graduate programs at the University of Pennsylvania and had been together for a semester in a course on group dynamics. There were six Elites, eight Middles, and ten Outs, and in most ways things started out in a form similar to Beacon Hill. However, this Lab ended in a very different way.

## Designing an Anti-Revolutionary System

The primary goal of the Farm Elites was to avoid a revolution. Initially they thought the best way to achieve this end was to make life as equitable as possible. They assumed the Outs would rebel. That led them to reason as follows:

> *We* must do the right thing or *they* will become criminals; *we* must make the system so equitable that *their criminality* and *subversive natures* will not be activated; *we* must seize power so it doesn't fall into the *hands of the irresponsible.*

The one thing the Farm Elites had in common was their shared angst about what would happen if power was in the wrong hands, and the "wrong hands" were anyone's but theirs. Their fear made it easy to agree about what to avoid but hard to concur on what to create.

Before the Outs reached the Farm, the Elites were convinced the powerless would hate them because they had power. They argued, "We must protect ourselves from the hostility the Outs will project onto us," without recognizing the hostile projections of the Elites contained in this view. Having agreed that all problems would be caused by the Outs, the Elites wanted to control their behavior and thought democracy was their best defense because any revolt by the masses would be a rebellion against themselves. These Elites concluded, "By placing the power in others' hands, we will not be blamed!" The Elites projected their own fears onto a group that still did not even exist, except in their imagination. They were frightened by the image they had constructed of the Outs.

While democracy promised a way to avoid revolution, it meant they would lose power, there being six Elites and eighteen others. So the Elites chose to form a Community Council with two representatives from each group, with the Elites having veto power on all decisions. They thought of this as power-sharing but failed to recognize how transparent this arrangement was to others.

Within the Elite group, decisions were made by consensus. This left no room for dissenting voices. However, one of their group, Blair, always took a different perspective from the other five. He saw his fellow Elites as only wanting to avoid conflict and thought this was not a good basis for decision making; but he could not get them to recognize this. Also, as they built their governance system, the Elites gave no thought to what the Middles might contribute or want, seeing them solely as a group that could be used to dampen the anticipated hostility of the Outs.

As they struggled with creating a democracy, the Elites functioned in highly undemocratic ways, refused to listen to their dissenting voice because he threatened consensus, and treated the Middles purely in utilitarian terms. Without realizing it, the Elites built into the DNA of their mini-society the things they most wanted to avoid: they wanted full participation, but squelched dissent; they wanted liberty for all, but bullied the Middles into a role they opposed. The Elites longed for everyone to be exactly what they were, so long as it was acceptable to the Elites.

Once the Elites learned the Outs were to be homeless, they threw themselves into a crisis management mode. Finding a solution to the homeless problem became their top priority. They rented from the conference center a shelter — a heated space with a carpeted floor, no beds, but enough blankets to keep the ten Outs warm, and lots of peanut butter, jelly, and bread. Providing this level of support for the Outs consumed 75 percent of the Elites' resources and severely limited their future options. However, it solved an immediate problem. The future seemed far off, and they believed this gave them a chance of avoiding an uprising on the first day.

## On Embracing Homelessness

After the Lab was over an Out gave the following description of their life as a group:

"We were registered the same night as the others but were kept in a classroom on campus and told to be ready to go at a moment's notice. By 2:00 a.m. we figured we would not depart until morning, so we slept on the floor. At 4:30, after a restless night, the registrar told us we were leaving in fifteen minutes. He escorted us to 30th Street Station and after a long wait told us to board the train pulling into platform D. He gave us each a ticket plus $2.70 for a bus fare and instructed us to get off at Norristown, catch the no. 33 to Crossroads, and walk to the point marked X on the map he gave us. Upon boarding the train we quickly galvanized as a group.

"It was a long journey. The last two miles walking in the bitter cold was particularly tough. We arrived at 10:00 a.m. As we went up the driveway to the Farm, someone quipped, 'Never have ten people worked so hard to get to a place they know they do not want to be,' and another said, 'We are looking for a place where we can feel at home, but I doubt if we have the capacity to recognize home when we see it.' We had yet to learn that we were to be homeless.

"Upon arrival we were taken to a shelter, two small rooms adjoined by a single bathroom. The floors were carpeted concrete and the ceilings were so low some of us could not stand upright. But things were better than we had expected. As we entered our shelter we ceremoniously took off our snow-clad shoes so that our beds, the floor, would not get wet. This was the first of many norms we established. The next thing we did was to urinate. It was hours since we'd seen a bathroom and the shelter had only one toilet. The question was asked, 'Who needs to go first?' This was our second norm: the most needy got priority. Our doors didn't lock but that didn't matter. We had nothing anyone could take. That was liberating. The only thing we could lose was our dignity, and that could not be stolen from us. It would vanish only if we gave it away.

"Early on we concluded we wanted adequate food and shelter, would oppose what others valued, and be as unpredictable as possible. We did not want to be institutionalized by others, but we were being so reactive we were institutionalizing ourselves. Later we had to free ourselves from this self-created bind.

"We Outs were a wild mixture: a fiery, Irish Catholic, who had been a truck driver, a union organizer, and a card-carrying member of the Teamsters; a Jewish woman from the upper class; an Indian male, a Brahman awakening to the effects of class and caste upon his identity and that of his people; one WASP; a Catholic woman who was an avowed feminist; a man all feminists want to change; an Asian American woman whose Taiwanese family immigrated to the United States when she was in high school; an Argentinean Jew who'd been trying to make a home for himself in Paris; a gay man, painfully open about his sexual orientation; and a man whose refugee family had come to the United States from Russia during his teens as they fled the horrors experienced by Soviet Jews.

"Many of us had strained relationships before the Lab, and it was hard to imagine this bunch of headstrong individuals could become a cohesive group. Also, men and women were living in close quarters, so bodily functions like urination and menstruation ceased to be private events.

"We chose to make decisions using what we called a 'round robin.' When we had to make a choice, one person would define the issue, and then each spoke in turn briefly about what he or she thought or felt. No one would repeat what another had said, but each was free to affirm or disagree with a previous statement. When all had spoken, the round robin cycled through a second or third time and each would express unspoken thoughts or feelings provoked by what others had said. During the recycling we often took positions different from our initial ones. Those with nothing to add said 'pass.' When everything had been stated, the group voted. A 70 percent majority constituted a decision. Once we made a decision we never went back on it. If a vote failed to get 70 percent the group reverted to the prevailing status quo.

"It took a while to become proficient at this process, but we eventually became masters at it. When something minor required attention we worked fast and came to a speedy conclusion. If we had a critical issue we took the time needed to consider everything fully. During our round robin we were not just making decisions, but were creating our group's character. We believed our shared integrity was our greatest asset. We had to nourish it. We treated each individual's view as important and changed our minds based on what others said. For us mind-changing was a strength and not a weakness. This helped us voice what we honestly thought and felt.

"Something else happened to us Outs. There was a quality to the conversations we were having that was unusual. As we spoke our minds we recognized there were many things we rarely gave voice to and that life might pass us by without our ever discovering what these unexpressed thoughts and feelings meant to us. So with everything that happened we told one another not only how it made us feel, but what aspect of life it helped shed light on. By the second day we were speaking with each other at a level of intimacy few had ever experienced.

"We saw the Elites as driven by the need to get rid of their guilt. So we adopted a stance of 'give us what we want and we won't make trouble for you.' That gave us some power but also created an unexpected consequence. We tried to improve our position by not improving our position, to undermine others by not undermining them. However, we soon found that we actually felt more fulfilled by not improving anything and not undermining anyone. So we chose to accept our Out status and forget about trying to be anything else, and we agreed to openly accept all gifts offered to us. This was a new experience for this bunch of individuals who believed that all progress depended on how well we fend for ourselves. We had never learned how to receive gifts others were willing to give us. We knew what money and ambition brought but had no clue about the treasures tucked inside impoverishment and surrender.

"After a while a subtle movement occurred in the Outs' way of being. We stopped basing our life on anyone else's terms, craving wealth and material possessions or being envious of those with resources. Instead we became grateful for all we had been given. This represented a sea change in our thinking. From then on, peanut butter and jelly sandwiches and a bedless shelter stopped being a sign of our homelessness and became a symbol of all the ways we were blessed.

"By the end of the first day at the Farm the Outs no longer cared about what the other groups did. We were existing fine and chose to spend our time examining what being homeless meant to us as human beings living in our particular world. For all of us, given what we expected out of life, the thing we feared most was having nothing and being nothing. Yet having nothing at the Farm left us no longer afraid of this possibility. We all craved to belong to a community, to have roots, yet we were all on journeys destined to create rootless lives. At the Farm we were learning what a remarkable community could be created by those who feel rootless.

"Our group was also falling in love, not romantic love, not Eros, but the form the Greeks called Agape, compassion for one another as valued members of the community. We became awash in Agape as we told one another what was in our hearts — the good, the bad, and the ugly."

## Pushed into a Buffer Role

This was how a Middle woman described their shared life at the Farm:

"We had so much diversity in our group it was hard to find common ground. The Middles had three women: two African Americans — one from the Deep South and one from the Northeast — and one Jewish woman. We had five men: an Afrikaner from Johannesburg, a Mormon from Middle America, a Jew from the Bronx, a Chinese American, and a black American born in Ethiopia and raised by a white family. However, upon meeting the Elites, we had a common experience of shock. They told us they would not ask the Outs to work because they did not want to alienate them and proceeded to tell us Middles that we had to do the menial tasks at the Farm to create resources to help feed the Outs. They did not seem to care how we felt.

"By the time we went to bed on the first night, the Middle men, outraged by the idea of working to get money to feed the Outs, wanted to revolt and unseat the Elites. But we Middle women were distressed by our men and their rebellious impulses, so we squelched them.

"The next morning the tension between the men and women in our group grew fierce. We women refused to do our assigned work but demanded the men do it so our group privileges would be preserved. We schemed among ourselves and were self-congratulatory when we conned the men into doing our bidding. The joint feelings we had about the men helped us three females to bond with one another. Meanwhile, our positions of 'we won't work but the men should' and 'we're against rebellion because we don't want to lose our privileges' led the men to believe that life would only improve for them if there was a full-blown social revolution.

"The Elites hoped we Middles would supervise the Outs and defined the Farm's goal as 'overcoming the debilitating effects of homelessness.' They wanted a program of 'cultural enrichment' so the Outs could be liberated from their emotional and intellectual impoverishment and be able to take their place as equals in the society. They asked that the society be governed by a Community Council with two representatives from each group.

"While we were not opposed to these ideas, we asked what would happen if we refused to do as the Elites decreed. The answer was the Middles could lose our meals and our beds. We proposed that the system be run on the 'one person, one vote' principle. Their response was we could suggest what we liked but we must use the Community Council as the vehicle for reform. However, capitulating to this demand would validate the very thing we wanted changed, but rebelling might make us Outs, so we went along with their scheme. That's how the Elites sucked us into the middle role.

"The Outs were pleased and surprised by how well they were cared for, but saw the Elites as easy to manipulate. They knew that the more pathetic they became, the more handouts they'd get, acquired of course by our Middle men who were doing the menial jobs so we Middle women would not lose our privileges. To be a mediating force we needed good relations with Elites and Outs; but we were shunned by the Outs and felt zero connection to the Elites or their goals.

"The most difficult thing for us, however, was that the men and women in our group could not agree on anything. The men wanted to displace the Elites and control the Farm, but we women blocked them. We were angry that our men made statements on behalf of all Middles without checking with us women to see what we thought. We were also convinced they would botch a coup attempt, resulting in all Middles losing our beds and meals. We also thought that being ruled by the Middle men would be worse than by the current Elites.

"For a while, the Outs sent representatives to the Community Council and were part of the Farm's governance, and we believed we were making progress. But the Council reinforced the differences among the groups: the Elites felt manipulated by the guilt-induction routines of the Outs, yet never acknowledged that they were trying to steer the other groups to do as they wished, namely, not to rebel; the Outs concluded that they were given things only because others were afraid they might disrupt Farm life and that they were being bought off as a way to preserve the status quo; the Middles wanted to democratize the system built on the 'one person, one vote' principle, but our group remained patriarchal with the Middle men making all decisions with no female input, while we women did endless covert things to undermine our men.

"During the Community Council meetings it was obvious how divided the Elites were. When one made a statement another would contradict it. Their attempts to clarify made the waters muddier. It was obvious the Elites were not up to the task of running this society. The problem was, who could do it? The Middles were the only serious alternative, but the Outs thought life would be no better under us. For them swapping rulers would advance nothing.

"On one occasion, all representatives at a Community Council meeting were women. This was not planned. It just happened. As we began, I noted the irony of having only women in this role at this time: the Farm society was bankrupt; when there were no resources left women were asked to sort out the mess. For a while the six female Council representatives debated what to do. But as we tried to deal with our bankrupt system, the Middle men interrupted repeatedly. We were furious that they would not be quiet. The meeting achieved nothing, in large part because the haves would not take responsibility for running the society. The Outs argued that the successes and the failures belonged to the haves. Their position was, 'We supported you as the rulers during the best of times, and now that it's the worst of times, you are still responsible. You can't pass your problems onto us. We are the Outs! That gives us the liberty of not having to worry about fixing a system we think is broken beyond repair.' In an instant our beliefs about what drove the Outs were shattered.

"We were upset that the Outs accepted their homeless state; we hoped they'd fight the Elites. What would we do with our rebellious energy when the Outs were unavailable to express it on our behalf? Would we battle with the Elites ourselves and risk losing all? Since the Elites and Middles had only one common purpose, keeping the Outs contained, we were confused about what to do. We had projected our hostility onto the Outs and were not happy with their cooperative spirit, because it meant we had to deal with our own hostility ourselves. We imploded and had a terrible fight. We women attacked the men for everything they had done and accused them of not being committed to the democracy they espoused; but we women had been silently undermining the men. Privately the men congratulated themselves on being liberated; but they saw us women as unwilling to do anything for anyone, which was true; but they never said a word of this to us women!"

## *Being a Recipient of Grace*

The Elites also imploded. This was how one of the Elites explained what transpired.

"When the Outs accepted their fate we should have celebrated; our goal of avoiding a revolution had been achieved, but our group was paralyzed by conflicts of our own and we were unhappy. The Elite group had a lot of diversity: two African Americans (a male and a female), two white men (a Jew and a Mormon), a blue-eyed blond woman, and a Japanese American woman. Initially our differences seemed irrelevant, but once we ceased to see the Outs as a threat we fell apart. First we attacked Blair, our dissident. He had asked us to look at how fear was driving our actions, but we were too scared of our privileges, too scared of failing, and too scared of being dethroned to embrace our fears. Blair made no suggestions about what to do, but he objected to every initiative we proposed. He stymied our group, and we tried to make him conform. But he refused to fit in. Actually he was only opposed to our unwillingness to examine why we chose the actions we did, but we never understood, even though he said it repeatedly.

"As Blair got increasingly out of synch with the rest of us, we worried about what he would do if he was in a position of power and there weren't people like us to keep him in check. We assumed he would become a mini-Hitler and unleash on others the negative energy we saw him expressing in our group. We thought this negativity was an attribute of his character, something he was born with or acquired during a bad childhood. We could not see that he was holding up a mirror to us, showing us something about our collective negativity. We saw him as a closet tyrant who would destroy the other groups just as he was ravaging ours. It never sunk in that his goal was to get us to examine our motives and to look at the inhumanity contained in what we were doing.

"At one point I'd had enough and turned on him: 'Blair, you often refer to yourself as our devil's advocate. Well, to hell with you! You *are* the devil in this group. Whenever we're close to doing something constructive you block us.' Yet the others and I had blocked as much as Blair. For all that frustrated us, we blamed Blair. But he refused to be silenced, and this infuriated us.

"We never noticed how our insistence on having consensus was impeding us, that our decision-making process gave each individual the ability to hold the group hostage. By refusing to agree, any of us could block action. We wanted to veto decisions other groups made that we didn't like. They rejected that. Yet each of us could veto an emerging decision in our group. Actually we all did this to ourselves often, but we got upset only when Blair tried to block us. Instead of altering how we made decisions, we rejected the one we saw as threatening our consensus.

"Blair knew we wanted him to be silent, but he refused. His position was, 'You can kick me out, but until I'm gone I will speak my mind!' This idea of throwing him out of the group planted a seed that germinated and grew. However, in the early days we needed Blair. He served as a kind of emotional garbage dump into which we could deposit our shared frustrations.

"There came a point when Blair privately decided to withdraw and became passive. During this time we made Blake, the other white male in our group, the focus of our anger. We accused him of being a wimp and not standing up to the other groups when they made demands on us, the very issue that had troubled Blair about all our behavior. For a while we Elite women blamed Blake for everything that had gone wrong, acting as if he had unilaterally made all our decisions. We flung expletive after expletive at Blake.

"Blair was relieved not to be the target of our anger for once. Had he tried to interrupt he'd have taken the brunt of it again. At the peak of the rage one of us argued, 'The only solution is to expel Blake from the Elites.' For a while it looked like this might happen. Then the one black man in our group moved to defend Blake. His move had a chilling effect on us and showed us women that we were the ones who were furious and were dumping our anger on the white men. Once it looked like we could have a male-female fight in our group I backed off. That was the last thing I wanted. However, the emotion in our group was like a hurricane whose fury was yet to be released.

"During the second day someone mentioned the names of the Middle men, and we Elite women exploded. We began by assassinating the characters of these men. Some of our attributions were extreme, such as 'Those guys and Hitler were cut from the same cloth' and 'I never realized that Elites had to protect society from little dictators who want to take control.' We had harbored similar thoughts of Blair. Could it be that we were seeing in the Middles things we felt about ourselves?

"When this emotional outburst ended we realized that our group was about to change in an unexpected way. Blair suddenly got up and left our group. We felt great relief.

"We eventually came to understand what happened to Blair. Shaken and disillusioned, he was sure the Middles would never accept him but he also did not want to be with them. He wanted to escape the struggles of the Farm and longed for a new resting place. The homeless shelter was his best option, so he went to ask the Outs if he could join them. He expected to be rejected. He did not see that having nothing and being eminently rejectable made him an Out by definition. He had no home, and hence no one could label him as 'not homeless.' The Outs' only choice was whether to welcome him into the shelter. Such irony: as an Elite, Blair owned the shelter; now he doubted if he'd be allowed to lay his head in it.

"With obvious pain, he told the Outs, 'I've left the Elites and want to ask if you'd let me be a part of your group.' The Outs were shocked but did not show it. Quickly one of them said, 'Before you enter please take your shoes off. To belong to us you must first humble yourself, and how we do this is to treat this grungy old floor as sacred ground.' Without a word Blair took off his shoes and sat on the floor. He had been in this shelter many times but had never removed his shoes. He had never considered that his snow-clad boots might make their bed, the warn-out carpet, so wet it would be impossible to sleep on. Nor had he ever sat on this floor, felt the cold of the concrete slab on his buttocks, or looked to human interaction to warm himself. One of the Outs told Blair that he had to understand that the physical conditions in the shelter were harsh and they had strict rules to help them cope. If he joined them he had to respect and abide by the Outs' rules.

"Blair was comforted to know there were rules to live by and clear consequences for his actions. It had frustrated him that the Elites acted as if they could do as they chose and experience no repercussions. It had felt tyrannical to have no rules and was liberating to be forced to respect some standards. Right away he recognized the Outs knew how to regulate their own behavior, something the Elites had yet to learn. The constraints and consequences had a calming effect on him. Blair told the group he had locked his possessions in an Elite car because he did not want to be different from the Outs. One of them gave him a little sermon: 'Blair, you'll always be different because you were an Elite and did not walk the same path as us to reach Outness. But you don't have to be the same as us to be an Out. We are all different! All Outs had a similar fate, but our pain is not the same. There is no rule saying our suffering must be identical. If you are in pain and have no place to stay, then you are homeless! Outs don't determine who is out. Others define that.'

"The Outs asked Blair to leave their shelter for a few minutes so that they could make their decision. They then proceeded with their round robin decision-making process. Several issues were raised. While it seemed dangerous to let Blair join them, they concluded they were strong enough to deal with any risk his presence posed. The main issue was that they had no right to turn anyone away from the shelter. It was public space provided for all who needed it. They were its current occupants, but that gave them no right to stop Blair from seeking refuge there.

"These ten Outs had traveled a long way from the Elite world they had left behind and to which they would return after the Lab. In the future many of them in regular life would make a mark on the world. However at the Farm they embraced the view that 'we are all but temporary occupants of this earth, and during the time we are here our task is to be faithful stewards of all we have been given. To fight over who actually owns this land would be as silly as two fleas on the back of an elephant arguing over who owns the elephant.'[11]

"The Outs saw themselves as living in an abundant world that had apportioned a little of its wealth to them, which they should share with all in need. They unanimously welcomed Blair as a full member of their shelter group. But they cautioned him: 'You have a lot of information that would be useful if we got in a fight with the Elites. However, we don't want you to say anything about what the Elites are planning. If you betray them that would compromise your integrity. If we asked you to compromise your integrity, we'd be inviting you to do something we would not do to ourselves. Please just share whatever you choose about your experience to date. That way the integrity of everyone will be maintained.'

"This was hard for Blair to hear. They had welcomed him and said, 'It is important to *us* that *you* preserve your integrity.' Blair, a despised Elite, was being offered a warm embrace. That took his breath away. He had never known what it felt like to be unconditionally accepted. He thanked them, but Blair's pent-up emotion overwhelmed him. The Outs were understanding and patient. When he regained his composure he asked, 'What is your strategy? I want to join in.' They roared with laughter: 'Our strategy is to never have a strategy. Right now we are going to play soccer. Please join us. Being Out is tough work, and we must play to preserve our sanity.' "

## Reinventing Society, Soviet Style

While the Elites and Middles lost focus, the Outs were feeling increasingly potent. The fact that Blair, an Elite, had joined them fueled a playful fantasy: 'Since we are the haven for all the discontents that don't fit in any more, in time we'll rule the world because they'll all be part of us.' This statement started as a court-jester type joke. However, the whole of the Farm society had grown so weak that the homeless group was its strongest component.

The final afternoon, the Outs allowed themselves to be pulled into a power game that they regretted. It started with a serious suggestion in response to an authentic question. The Elites wanted to know how the Outs had built such a sense of solidarity. They responded, "The best way to learn that is to walk a mile in our shoes." The Elites asked, "How could we do that?" The Outs glibly replied, "Come and eat sandwiches with us and sleep in our shelter." This was not meant to be taken seriously. No Out wanted the haves sleeping on the floor with them. But the Elites said, "Okay, we will join you in the shelter for the night!" Before the Outs could stop it, a new movement had begun: 'Let's empathize with the downtrodden!' In a flash they had the Elites' syrupy empathy and felt sickened by it. The Outs just wanted to be left alone. Soon all remaining Elite and Middle meals that had already been paid for were canceled, and in their place extra peanut butter and jelly sandwiches were ordered for all. And twenty-four people prepared to cram themselves for a night into a shelter that could accommodate no more than twelve.

The Outs won a moral victory, but the haves were treating it like a one-night stand, an evening field trip, an opportunity to camp out with the homeless. For the Outs, having the Elites and Middles walking into, around, and through their inner sanctum felt debasing.

> *I am weary with my groaning.*
> *All night long I water my bed with my tears.*
>
> Psalm 6:6

# Chapter 4

# Dancing with Shadows

## On Reflection

Upon the conclusion of the Lab at Fellowship Farm the participants and staff spent two days reviewing what had transpired over the previous sixty hours. We explored what had happened in relationships among the three groups, what had gone on within each group, and ultimately what had been activated inside each person. We soon realized there had been Power Labs occurring at three different levels. First, there was the system-as-a-whole Lab, defined by the tussles among the Elites, the Middles, and the Outs. However, within the ranks of these three groups there had also been a constant struggle between people who occupied positions of power, of powerlessness, or of being caught in the middle. So a second set of Labs were those that had taken place *inside* each group. Then there were the Power Labs raging *within each participant,* as each tried to manage the part of the self that felt powerful, the part that felt powerless, and the part that was trapped in the psychological void between these internal polarities.

As we moved to this third level of analysis the emotional fireworks began. Intellectual vistas flung open and a spirit of possibility, hope, and renewal rushed into dark corners desperate for sunlight. Each person scrutinized the parts of the self that made it so hard to be "at home," both with one's emotions and with the external world. And in this place of not feeling at home we found access to a source of power much larger than ourselves and became joyful in ways that had previously seemed elusive. We also learned that our investment in not being vulnerable had stopped us from seeing the many emotional and spiritual

43

supports available to us that would have removed many of our vulnerabilities had we accepted what we were: lost people craving a place where we felt at home. Alas, the methods we had used to protect ourselves had made us more vulnerable than if we had never tried to insulate ourselves from harm.

Most members of this community had grown up expecting that feelings of self-worth and efficacy would come by climbing to high places, by accumulating wealth, by being someone important. In the days following the Lab they found that by embracing what they had most wanted to avoid they gained what their hearts had yearned for. Paradoxically, they became more at home within themselves as they let go of lofty aspirations and saw value in the downward journey.

Many of the participants longed to be in a place where they felt complete, where they could see the interconnectedness of all things, where there was no urgency to rush to a different place. This reminded me of the universal wish to be in "heaven" and also confronted me with my reluctance to be fully present in any moment, to allow the holism of everything to sink in, to celebrate the life-sustaining energies that help me rise at dawn and rest at nightfall. I soon realized that if I were in heaven and insisted on remaining as I am — since heaven is a way of being rather than a place — I actually would not be in heaven because I would be unable to experience it as heaven.[12] Perhaps heaven is so hard to achieve on earth because people have to give up too much. It is hard to live with hearts exposed; it is hard not to blame others for the apparent adversities of our lives! The Tibetan Book of the Dead suggests we are on the path to heaven when we learn to see the divine in others, our adversaries included, which ultimately points us to the divinity in the self. Had these young men and women gone to the Farm in search of the part of heaven planted in them at birth?

The revitalizing insights about the search for a sense of home tapped by the Farm community constitute the core of what is to come. However, to create a structure for exploring this material we briefly reflect on the Lab at the system-as-a-whole level and the Labs within each of the groups.

# The Construction-Destruction-Integration Triangle

During the review session the Farm participants recognized that their interactions were driven by the same construction-destruction-integration dynamics that had dominated Beacon Hill. At the Farm things began the same way: the Elites wanted to construct a mini-society where everyone felt they belonged, and the Outs wanted to rebel against the expectations of others. However, the Middles remained in the mediating, in-between position and never sided with the Elites or the Outs. They stayed squarely in the middle. This had a huge impact. The Elites' posture of "we *will* create the world we *want*" remained connected to the position of the Outs, which was "we don't like your world and *reject* it because we are determined to shape our own destiny." Although the Middles were not consciously trying to be the yoke binding the haves and the have-nots to each other, the Middles' actions did keep these polar perspectives coupled. This helped the Outs to conclude that fighting with the Elites was futile and to give over to being what they were, the disenfranchised.

As at Beacon Hill, the tugs over constructive, destructive, and integrative energies were seen in the Farm Elites' wish to build a system the Outs would not want to destroy and in the Outs' initial intent to suck the haves dry and weaken their power base. They were also evident in how the Middles buffered the tensions between the haves and have-nots. Their version of democracy kept these polarities connected and helped the Farm system to function, at least in a rudimentary way.

# The Power Lab Occurring within Each Group

The same construction-destruction-integration triangle was evident within each of the three groups. This was most obvious in the behavior of the Outs. Typically, groups with little or no power dump their angry and vengeful feelings on the powerful. However, the Farm Outs concluded that the Elites were doing the best they could, given their resources and the system they had inherited. So when they were distressed by the actions of the Elites, the Outs did not blame them or rise up in protest, but just debated what was the best way to deal with the situation. This was not easy because they had to manage many constructive and destructive energies that erupted within their own group. However, in the shelter those adopting a constructive stance on one issue were often the ones taking a destructive posture on the next, and vice versa. The Outs also took turns mediating their own disputes. Hence none of them got locked into the position of constructor, destroyer, or mediator. Individuals rotated into and out of these functions as the situation demanded; no one was captive to any of the internal roles temporarily adopted on behalf of everyone.

Within a day, the Outs had discovered how to maintain their vitality even in the midst of considerable turbulence: they considered negative energy as normal and did not dismiss it as aberrant; they treated their destructive impulses as expressions of their own internal dynamics and did not displace them onto others; they focused on what they could create and did not let minor setbacks drain them of important energies; they valued all voices and made sure no one was silenced; they encouraged members to be flexible and did not demand that people be consistent from one event to the next; they viewed unpredictable behavior as mere fluctuations and did not characterize anyone as being chaotic; they built connections between opposing positions in their group; and they did not let disputes fragment them. The Outs' ability to remain in touch with both their own destructive and constructive energies gave them considerable vivacity. They did not run from troublesome feelings in their group, nor did their group project feelings of self-contempt onto others. The Outs were able to draw upon the power that came from their constructive, their destructive, and their integrative parts. They did their own work to keep themselves integrated.

In comparison, the Elite group was torn asunder by its inability to keep its constructive and destructive sides linked. It too had an internal battle between the powerful and powerless facets of itself. Five of the six Elites tried to bring their vision for the Farm to fruition, while Blair acted to block them. He fought against everything the other Elites wanted, not because he disagreed with their goals, but because he thought they were doing it for the wrong reasons. Disturbed by his opposition, the other Elites turned against him. Blair tried to help his peers see that they were driven by their collective fear that the Outs might rebel. He felt the Elites wanted to preemptively destroy those who might wish to destroy what the Elites hoped to construct, namely, a mini-society with no destructiveness or rebellion. The other Elites felt that Blair undermined them at every turn and construed their motives as dishonorable so he could seize the moral high ground. Blair thought he was just asking his group to acknowledge honestly that its primary motive was to avoid conflict and to prevent revolt. The Elites had no members occupying the middle ground who could be an integrating force and pull the oppositional energies together or ameliorate the group tensions resulting from those polarities.

Many of Blair's actions helped keep the Elites on track, but the more he stated his views the stronger their contempt for him grew. The situation became intolerable, and he left. For a while the Elites dared to believe that its demonic force had gone. But with Blair's departure the Elite group lost contact with its own destructive side and was soon seeing the actions and the character of the Outs and the Middles in demonic terms.

The Middle group had similar power dynamics within its own ranks. While the Middles worked hard to pull Elites and Outs into the system of governance they hoped to install, they could not keep their own group unified. Their "one person, one vote" posture, repeated again and again like a social mantra, did provide some social cohesion for the whole system and helped to sustain critical dialogue when conflictual interactions could have spiraled out of control. However, the Middle group itself was always straining at the seams. The men from the Middles argued that democracy was the best way to keep the Farm from splintering, but they alienated the women in their group by behaving autocratically. These men said they wanted to make the Farm a better place for all, but the Middle women did not believe they could deliver on such a promise and formed themselves into a covert resistance movement. The conflicts within the Middles degenerated into classic gender battles. Having no subgroup within its ranks able to occupy the center and keep their fighting factions integrated, the Middle group got stuck and lost its potency.

The effectiveness of both the Elites and the Middles was hindered by their inability to internally integrate the constructive and destructive energies that existed within their respective groups. In contrast, the Outs managed to sustain the coexistence of these opposite sides of themselves. It kept polarized positions and contradictions connected and did not become paralyzed. The Outs even derived strength from their internal struggles. However, the fighting among the internal factions of the other groups drained them of their energies and left them depotentiated.

## The Power Lab within Each Individual

When the review shifted to how each person's internal functioning was like a Power Lab, the following questions were asked: What is the Elite part of us like? What do we do with our constructive energies? What form does the Out part of us take? How do our destructive energies get enacted? What does our middle, integrating self attend to and how does it keep the polarities connected? Does our internal Middle try to tone down the Elite and Out selves so the tensions between them do not escalate? Does the Middle self try to amplify, lessen, contain, or release the energies latent in the opposite parts of the self?

During this portion of the review the Outs exploded with enthusiasm. They spoke about how much they had connected with one another as have-nots, how comforting their period of homelessness had been, and how upset they were when it was time to leave their shelter. The others did not understand what had been special about being powerless, so the Outs told them. This opened up many new themes. Soon the Elites and Middles joined in and spoke about the ways they too felt *emotionally homeless* in the larger world and how much they ached for a new way of being. During our two-day review, the spirit that had been born in the shelter grew until everyone in the community was affected by it.

These conversations showed us that the inner landscape of each person was a microcosm of both the within- and between-group processes experienced at the Farm, and the many family, group, organizational, and communal dynamics of life in general. This parallelism was fascinating, and soon we recognized how many of the things swirling around inside us were like a shadow play of our external worlds. We had never appreciated how much our inner turmoil resulted not from intrapsychic issues, but from our inability to block out social despair, communal turbulence, and a plethora of things that should never be allowed to enter the human heart. Nor had we previously cherished all the valuable gifts offered to us by that external world.

While members of the Farm community had previously known very little about the ways their inner beings were linked to external forces, they had all carried some clues about this reality. For example, they held the view that when they wanted things to be different, their best hope was to get the external dynamics within which they lived to change. And having all worked hard at some point to alter dynamics in their families, their workplaces, their relational networks, they knew first-hand the frustrations of not succeeding. Having failed to change those outside forces, these men and women felt destined to remain captive to them, so they were quite excited to find that the key to their own liberation resided inside themselves. They had been invested in changing the external, hoping that this would make their internal beings different, but they had not considered altering themselves directly.

To their astonishment they discovered that as they began changing the self, their experience of the external altered, which led them to interact with the external differently. Then their own changed behavior, driven by who they were becoming and not by the need to make the exterior different to satisfy some needs of their own, actually altered the external dynamics that had been so troublesome. In the past they had fought against becoming what the outside was forcing them to be, and that had left them paralyzed. When they accepted that fighting the external only made it more powerful and they replaced combativeness with a quiet acceptance of what was going on within, they discovered a well-spring of change possibilities that made the outside seem momentarily less relevant. By taking back the power they had previously given to the external, their experience of the external altered dramatically.

While working to grasp these new perspectives, Farm participants saw the self as carrying an Elite, an Out, and a Middle within. They also appreciated that the struggles among the parts of the self were similar to the interactions within and among the three groups.

## The Creative-Suffering-Accepting Self

Given their life trajectories, members of the Farm community were well aware of the Elite part of them, which we labeled the "creative self" to avoid being caught in the conceptual trappings of social class. Each person, whether poor or rich, educated or illiterate, hopeful or desolate, has a creative self. This is the part of the self that generates the activities and products from which the corpus of a life is constructed. Society validates the creative self, so long as its fecundity adds to the social fabric. Everyone at the Lab was attracted to this creative, elite part of them and was grateful for the privileges the external world had bestowed upon them, although they did not say this aloud for fear of being labeled proud, ambitious, pampered, or elitist. Nevertheless, the fact that they were graduate students in an Ivy League institution indicated that they were highly invested in this facet of the self and that they possessed the creativity society valued.

Yet they also knew something was missing. They all had an unarticulated longing and were engaged in a search for something that seemed too elusive to name, too nebulous to grasp. They wanted a different take on life and believed that by pursuing their creative potential, by striving harder, by broadening their horizons, they would find what they lacked. They did not think that embracing their destructive propensities, giving up their ambitions, and narrowing their fields of vision would bring them closer to what they sought. However, many recognized that they needed to learn about the disenfranchised and invalidated parts of themselves. Half of the participants had even expressed the hope that they would be Outs, stating clearly their wish "to rip everything down and make things better by rebuilding." This wish revealed their fantasy that the Outs have the best take on "how things ought to be," and that "the elite in them" would be more effective if it could absorb what the "out in them" understood. We chose the term "suffering self" for the "internal out" in each person. It is the place where individual angst is stored and from which emanates the pain that fuels the rebellious and "let's rip down the world" impulses all possess in good measure.

Life in the shelter was harsh, and the Outs gained relief by telling personal stories that exposed their woundedness. By a process that was hard to identify, their conversations about the parts of them that seemed irreparable, ugly, and unacceptable nourished them, both individually and collectively. They also acknowledged how much they were motivated by the Out in them, the part of the self that felt undeserving of all they had been given. During these storytelling times they discovered together their suffering selves, and to their delight found they were accessing a kind of loving often referred to as compassion, a term that at its root means "actively sharing in one another's suffering."

As participants told their stories, it was obvious that each was keenly aware of the suffering self, although it was normally kept private and was overshadowed by the creative self, which they were pleased to show in the public arena. However, it was hard for them to integrate the seemingly opposing energies produced by their creative and suffering selves. Using the Power Lab language, they did not have a strong enough Middle to keep their internal polarities integrated.

The Farm community worked on enabling the suffering and creative selves to live side by side. Often the energies of one seem to cancel out the vitality of the other, so the question is how to integrate the creative and suffering selves without having one overshadow or invalidate the other. If both these selves are allowed to fully be what they are, the conflicts can be extreme, making the risk of internal fragmentation high. Since these two selves are normally in opposition, the inner life certainly seems less chaotic when each is modified or reduced by the other. Yet forcing either the creative or the suffering self to be something other than what it is makes meaningless the minimal integration gained by dampening down the conflicts.

Throughout the review we asked the question, What was our Middle, our integrating self, actually doing? Most people's personal Middle turned out to be functioning like a stifling self, an avoiding self, an invalidating self. It did not work to integrate the creative and suffering selves but tried to ameliorate the tensions that existed between them by squelching each self. To the creative self it said, "Do not let loose with your full potential. It is too threatening." This voice prompted these individuals who dreamed big to actually live small. It dissuaded them from constructing lives that came close to fulfilling their potential and led them to moan about all that was wrong with their existence. To the suffering self the Middle said, "Life is not as bad as you claim. Look at all you have. There are many who are worse off but don't complain. Get a grip and stop blaming others for what goes wrong." The Middle selves had been telling the suffering selves that the pain being felt was not real. The result? The part of the self that already felt invalidated was negated even more.

In general, the Middle self, instead of working to provide inner integration, tried to alleviate the tensions between the creative and suffering selves by processes such as fleeing, stealing, projecting, imploding, and hiding. While these actions provided temporary relief, they did not bring the suffering and the creative selves together, but fostered the very fragmentation that produced the experience of emotional homelessness.

The Middle self needed a new way to function. In our Lab community when the Middle self became an "accepting self," many things altered in a positive direction. A sense of internal integration became possible as the Middle self accepted that the creative and suffering selves were both each other's opposite and each other's complement, that they were like the light and the dark, simultaneously co-defining each other and making the existence of the other possible. As an individual's Middle became an accepting self, old feelings about not being at home within oneself lessened dramatically.

However, moving to a place of self-acceptance was not easy. For those whose Middle selves were caught in the dynamics of fleeing, stealing, projecting, imploding, or hiding, acceptance was not accomplished solely on the basis of their own individual energies. What happened collectively proved to be a major determinant of both the character and the extent of individual change. The shift in the community of relations both at the Farm and during the review process was critical. Without that collective movement, individual shifts would not have occurred so quickly and for so many. Of course, as the individuals changed, this made the community a richer container for the angst all felt as they ventured into new and scary territory.

This highly supportive community of relations did not magically appear. It came about because of the actions of those who courageously shared all of who they were. Paradoxically, the sharing of suffering selves created the emotional safety all needed in order to share those suffering selves. Also, by allowing those suffering selves to be fully what they were, the creative self got stronger, which, of course, increased the need for a more robust accepting self.

With these frames in place, we now turn to the lessons learned together as the triumvirate of our creative-suffering-accepting emerged from the darkness and entered the spotlight.

> *How long must I suffer anguish in my soul*
> *and grief in my heart?*
>
> Psalm 13:2

# Chapter 5

# *Celebrating Our Brokenness*

The following stories of Daniel, Arun, and Blair place the theme of brokenness into the forefront of our consciousness. These three men had the posture of the self-assured, the demeanor of guys going places. There was no doubt that they would leave their mark. Yet each had an internal sense of the self that was out of synch with his public persona and an inner space that was dominated by a dreaded darkness. They had tried to drive the gloom away, but failed. During their visit to the Farm and the review session that followed the Lab, they discovered the centrality of the suffering self and the powerful role the shadows played in keeping the soul vibrant.

Latania, an African American woman, also entered center stage. In contrast to the men, she had the deportment of a person who would never "get it together." But this woman exuded a quiet confidence that others envied. She seemed internally unburdened, but alas, her public ways of being prompted others to reject her.

Historically, these four individuals had dealt with the contradictions that came from the clashes between their creative and their suffering selves by fleeing. However, the energy it took to remain in flight was draining them. In the near future it seemed that they would be forced to make tradeoffs between their bountiful potential, which their creative selves suggested they possessed, and the limits of their endurance, which their suffering selves insisted on pointing out.

As we listened to these individuals, it was evident that their inner struggles paralleled the dynamics operative in the Lab-as-a-whole. The Elite part of them was at war with the Out part of them, and the Middle part of them could no longer hold the center. But fleeing from this inner tension offered only short-term relief. Their ways of trying to shed their afflictions only intensified the problem. During the review session they stopped running.

Their stories, along with a fragment of my own struggles to find an emotional home, illustrate how our historical brokenness can serve as a guide in the search for renewal.

## Daniel: Singing in a Foreign Land

All my life I have felt not-at-home and have assumed that there must be a place where I will feel accepted. At the Farm I found it. Being an Out was comforting, calming, and energizing. Who would have guessed this would happen in a bedless, damp, concrete-floored shelter that no person would choose to call home!

This experience gave me a new perspective on myself. I saw reflected back a twenty-eight-year-old in quiet despair over never having felt accepted. I had always tried to mask my fears by frenetically searching for a place where I would not feel scared. Ironically, when I let myself be petrified, I found a way to be unafraid. That helped me to stop running from my fears. When I accepted that my dread was real, the energies I put into blocking my feelings were released and became available for other pursuits.

My parents and grandparents' family fled Nazi Germany and ended up in Argentina. They worked to make a place for themselves in South America, but it never really felt like home to me. Had it not been for the accidents of history that brought Hitler to power and destroyed European Jewry, my parents would still be in Hamburg. For reasons I never grasped, I always saw it as my job to reverse this mistake of history and to reestablish my family's place in Europe. I had to right wrongs that were done before I was born.

For as long as I could remember I sensed I had come from somewhere else. My family lived in a German- and Spanish-speaking area, and the people who lived nearby treated me as different. Because I was Jewish I was defined as a minority. On entering compulsory military service I was even investigated and then given jobs kept for political activists, criminals, and Jews.

At twenty-one I visited Israel. This changed me. Standing on that ancient soil I understood why I, and all my forefathers back to the first Hebrews, were so preoccupied with the issue of home. For a while I contemplated living in Israel, but I never moved there. However, visiting Israel set me on a journey. I had hoped it would soon end. Now I think it will last until the end of my days.

It was inevitable that I would leave Argentina. At fourteen, I gave my mother a prayer book with the inscription, "May this book stay by your side even though I myself might one day be far away." I did not know why I wanted to leave, but my desire to flee Argentina was deeply rooted in my family of origin. We all wanted to be gone from a place that would never let us fully be who we were. My leaving was not just for me but for all of them.

I headed for Europe and settled in Paris. As I boarded the plane, my father told a friend, "My son will never come back." He was right. After a tumultuous first year I built a network of friends, learned the language, and adapted to the culture, much as the Hebrews of old had done in Egypt. I secretly began to feel France was a place I would someday call home. However, I knew the French would never treat me as one of them. I had watched my parents fail in their attempt to become Argentinean, and I knew my fate could be the same. Being in Paris helped me be less anxious, but it also made me aware of how much of a misfit I was; it was easier dealing with not belonging when it was obvious to all that I didn't fit in. When others assumed I belonged and I didn't, it was torture.

After a few years I came to the United States for graduate school. I befriended only the French and refused to connect with Argentineans or Americans. I clung tenaciously to my newly acquired French identity. However, this made me once again an Out, this time in America. My way of being in each new location meant I was acquiring more and more places where I felt like an Out.

I always assumed I would return to France and continue my life there. This was not to be. At the Farm I stopped running from my fears and confronted my ambivalence about being settled anywhere. I realized that I wanted to both settle down and not settle down at the same time. That insight showed me that my search for a home was but a smoke screen. The real question was whether I could find a way to be at home with myself, no matter where I was. This was the fresh perspective I needed.

Instead of being frightened by the Out part of me, I began to celebrate its existence. I caught a glimpse of how wonderful being an outsider can be and how torturous it often is for the insider. I also saw how rigidly I viewed the world. My habit of treating things as black or white had made me feel secure but had also trapped me. It was scary letting go of firmly held convictions, but this was the change I needed to make. In a visceral way, I grasped the transitory nature of my existence.

I now know my task is less about finding a physical place where this Jew can be at home, and more about how to be at home with my Jewishness. Of late I have seen my life as an inverted tree, with the branches in the ground and the roots in the sky. Both my sense of home and my nomadic nature are embedded in my Jewishness, and no soil has ever been able to contain that. Being Out has kept my Jewish identity alive. It was such a relief to accept what I had avoided for so long: that to ground my sense of home in a physical location would detract from finding how to be at home in my spirit.

I have become increasingly drawn to the imagery provided in the Jewish observance of Sukkoth, a celebration of the harvest. For a week Jews live in cabins with an open roof to receive the sunshine by the day and see the stars during the night, where the clouds provide daytime shade and evening warmth. I have grown to love this commemoration of the Hebrews' wandering in the desert after fleeing Egypt. It symbolizes that our concrete houses cannot protect us, for only the Eternal is real. These temporary huts remind us how ephemeral life is, heighten the poignancy of our existence, and help us celebrate the journey.

To my surprise, I decided to remain in the United States. If I returned to France I would be pursuing an illusion. I have accepted that I will feel at home in my spirit only when I acknowledge how uncertain, afraid, and lost I feel in this world. This is a lesson the Jews came to understand on their long journey to the Promised Land. I accepted a job in Washington, D.C., a city populated by people coming or going. I will be a wanderer among other nomads.

## Arun: Darkness Is No Darkness

Early in this course I saw no relevance in what we were doing. I liked my classmates but detested the laborious way they addressed things that deserved only a superficial treatment. I coped by taking all meaningful thoughts and trivializing them. This mirrored my life as a whole. My wife and I had been in this country for three years, but the culture remained a mystery to us and we refused to be part of it. We longed for India, the sights, sounds, and tastes of the familiar, but I was here because I never fit in there. I hated being a foreigner, but that was a small part of my dilemma.

The moment came when I could contain myself no longer, and I blurted out that I felt lost in this course and hated the attendant feelings. Others seemed to appreciate my honesty, but no one would go near my emotions. That was fair enough. I couldn't deal with them so why should they? They were at a loss about what to do with my lostness. I felt better being honest about my terror, but worse because my fears seemed to make them more cautious about me. I felt like an ogre.

As we left for the Farm it was a different story. While my worries had been growing, so had everyone else's, and we were all in the same boat. I could not have been happier that first night when we concluded we were the Outs. I was a misfit in this class, a misfit in this culture, and a misfit in India too. Although I am a Brahmin and supposedly a member of the upper crust, I have never felt I belonged in India. And since being in the United States and getting some perspective on my heritage, I doubt if I could return to the life that had been scripted for me.

At the end of the long walk that brought us to the Farm, I said, "We have worked very hard to get to a place none of us want to be." I was talking about the Farm, but it fit the larger realities of all our lives in general. What was I doing at Wharton? I did not really want to be a businessman. What was I doing in America? I had no wish to be an international leader, the supposed reason I had come to graduate school. I had no idea of who I was or what I wanted. I was exhausted trying to meet others' expectations of me. I had filled my life with their aspirations because I did not have any of my own.

I was surprised that being homeless could be so liberating. At the beginning I was apprehensive, as were all the Outs. We were battling our fears. As I look back, however, I can see that this was the first time in my life where my role, my position, my status, let me just *be*. There was nothing required of me, nobody to please or displease. We were the Outs, and even if others were displeased, that was okay because it was our destiny to be the "displeasing ones." There was nothing they could take from us. We had nothing others wanted! I thought our desire for a warm bed and food would be so strong we would revolt. The opposite happened. We had a cozy shelter, peanut butter and jelly sandwiches, and not a care in the world.

All my life I have felt imprisoned by the demand to live up to other people's expectations; "be intelligent," "work hard," "be successful" had been drilled into me from childhood. Well, I did not feel intelligent, rarely worked hard, and never felt successful at anything. Others' views of me and my take on myself were way off. At the Farm, my internal and external realities were congruent. For once I was not living a lie; it felt wonderful to accept that I did not belong in the mainstream.

The strength and cohesion of the Outs, in large part, emerged because we felt not-at-home in real life. Some of us were foreigners and had stories about how we did not fit in. However, the Americans also seemed emotionally alienated too. We found the homeless part of each of us and shared it with such intimacy, acceptance, and warmth that we no longer felt homeless. We found in our homelessness the very thing we always hoped home would give us.

During our time together, we told each other the stories of our lives and discovered they were identical. We were at a prestigious university, on the verge of careers that would make us the elites of the world, and yet we felt completely lost. We pretended we had it together, that we knew what we were doing. This was a lie. It was therapeutic to admit to each other just how lost we felt in real life. That's what made our group so cohesive, getting honest with each other.

I felt empathy for the Elites and Middles who tried so hard to act as if they knew what they were doing. We knew they were as lost as us, and that there was no point following them. Those poor souls were in the worst position because they could not even admit to themselves, let alone anyone else, that they had no idea what to do with the supposed power they had. That is why it was easy to accept Blair into our midst. He had decided to stop living the same lie we had abandoned only a couple of days earlier.

I always claimed my feelings resulted from being a foreigner, but I've been a lost soul no matter where I am. The real issue is I've always been an alien to myself. I *hated* America, India, in fact everywhere I'd been, because I've *hated* the feelings I had about myself. I'm always in the midst of foreigners, not because of who is around me, but because of who I am. Every place is foreign to me because I am a stranger to myself. However, it seems easier to say "I'm an outsider" in a place where I clearly am an outsider than to try to live in a place where it is assumed I am on the inside but am not.

I was surprised to see the power of guilt at work and how much it messed us up. We Outs were very effective using guilt induction as a weapon. We enjoyed every moment of it and milked it for all it was worth. As we learned how vulnerable the other groups were, they put more and more power into our hands and were sitting ducks for our guilt-induction routines.

Guilt has played a big role in my personal history. I carry a lot of it in me and that makes me easy to manipulate. Further, when I do things to lessen my guilt, I feel resentful. Where does my guilt come from? First, I feel guilty about being a man. When I think of all the awful things we men have done to women across time, I feel ashamed. Trying to rid myself of these guilt feelings shapes my interactions with my wife, and it is destructive; I'm often caught between what I want to do and what I think I should do. When I choose the latter it is only because I can't stand myself if I don't; I overcompensate to deal with my guilt and end up feeling unhappy and resentful. I also feel guilty about not being in India to care for my parents as they get older. But if I were to return to India it would be to avoid feeling guilty about not going back. Then I'd be caring for them not out of love, but to appease guilt. How valuable would my guilt-riddled care be? Only love heals, and I cannot access feelings of love when I feel guilty about not caring for them, as I believe I should.

At the Farm I saw that genuine love is beyond guilt. That's the path I am now on. The first step was admitting to myself that I am a lost soul, that I am not at home with myself. Strangely, that acknowledgment alone has brought an inner acceptance I never had.

## *Blair: Running Wild at Nightfall*

I started Farm life as an Elite; I ended it as an Out. What a turn of events! I was excited to be an Elite. I had many things I wanted to explore and to learn. I hoped to create something new. This put me at odds with the other Elites, who seemed invested only in avoiding a rebellion. To achieve this end, they gave away the few possessions we had. I thought these material things were only a symbol of power; they were not much use, in and of themselves. We managed to contain the Outs' unrest but created little of value. I felt extremely alienated as an Elite. When I could stand it no longer, I left and joined the only group that I thought would have me: the Outs.

That was one wild and crazy group. They were wonderful to me. I had hit rock bottom, and for them that made me an Out. I thought they would reject me because I was the enemy. Wrong! They did not think in terms of allies and enemies. Only those invested in the pursuit of power reason that way. The Outs did not want power. They were focused only on how to get their next meal and whether their actions increased or decreased their solidarity.

They accepted me because it was their nature to do so. In spirit I was always one of them, for I was an Out among the Elites. How the Outs treated me was unrelated to what I had done or to my character. They accepted me because I was a misfit and all misfits belonged in their midst.

I never dreamed that the acceptance I craved would be available in the Outs. It was my wish to be found acceptable that made me want to be Elite. I thought that if I was in power I could make the rules by which one got acceptance. Then I could mandate the acceptance I craved. How wrong I was! My wish to control everything ensured the nonacceptance I wished to avoid. The Outs' acceptance spun me around like a toy top and set me in a new direction.

Joining the Outs caused me to revisit some dark times I wanted to leave behind. I was a man with a black hole at the center of my being. It was eating away at me. Some unknown monster had control of my soul, and I had no idea how to free myself from the grip it had on me.

It all came to a head as the Farm society ended. At daybreak, in preparation for the review session, we were asked to take a long walk alone, to notice the beauty of nature surrounding us and open ourselves to the fresh possibilities the new dawn might bring. I had awoken with a whirlwind of feelings. I was about to face the other Elites for the first time since migrating and was still furious at them. I thought all my feelings were solely about what had happened at the Farm. I did not recognize that I'd brought most of these emotions along with me from the rest of my life.

The moment I heard the invitation to go for a walk alone I was off. It started as a gentle jog and soon became a fierce run. The tears came right away as the pain from feeling an outcast caught up with me. As the emotions got more and more intolerable, I ran faster. I wanted desperately to be gone from everything, most of all myself. In time I was totally exhausted. That jolted me into the most intense period of isolation I have ever experienced. My wish to never return overwhelmed me.

Approaching the limit of what my body could tolerate, I saw the folly of trying to outrun the problems haunting me. My athletic capabilities were no match for what I wanted to flee. And of course, all these problems resided in me, no one else. Wherever I went, they traveled with me. Trying to outsprint my disturbance had been a lifelong habit. I'd used every form of flight known to escape my inner demons, but none of them worked: not drugs, not my rock and roll band, not sport, not education, not therapy. My cures had only bound me more fiercely to all I wanted to avoid.

I stumbled into a wire fence that marked the perimeter of the Farm. I crossed it, my destination obscure. I slowed. Sheltered by the thicket of the woods, I sat on a log. Initially, I did not know what I was running from. Why did I flee the Farm when invited to open myself to the acceptance the Outs had given me? Fortunately, I had run as far and as fast as my body could carry me. Reaching my limits put me so close to the edge, something had to give.

After my sweat dried and the chill penetrated my bones, I started my slow trek back to the Farm community, knowing I had to confront what I had been avoiding all my life. I did not think I had what it took to do this alone, and I was anxious about what was ahead. I had to find a way to be still, to look into the face of all that troubled me about myself, to make peace with who I am.

Upon my return I was stunned by the level of acceptance that surrounded me. I felt I had nothing to offer anyone. All I had was my spent self. It turned out that this was all I needed. It did not matter to others how troubled I was, how messed up my life had got, or how much I had wounded them in my mad frenzy to control my world. They accepted me just as I am and let me know that this could be a time of new beginnings for me, if I so chose.

During the review period I sat silently and listened with newly calibrated ears. I took in their experiences on their terms instead of my own. In time, the reverberations in my own head subsided and I stopped focusing on myself. What mattered to others began to matter to me. The grief of the gay man in our midst whose partner was dying of AIDS was my grief also. The anguish of the African American woman in our midst whose dad had disowned her because of her love for a white man was my anguish also. The pain of the Afrikaner in our midst who had seen for the first time the depth of his racism on the cusp of his return to his native South Africa was my pain also. I grasped what John Donne meant when he said, "Any man's death diminishes me for I am involved in mankind. Therefore never ask for whom the bell tolls, it tolls for thee."

My turmoil was certainly of my own making. However, I was not the only one affected by it. The people around me were also affected by my condition. Their renewal was having an effect on me. Maybe if I got myself fixed up, it might ultimately benefit them too!

When my peers let me see their full selves, their luminescent and their dark sides, I knew that they fully accepted me. When you show all of yourself to people, you are telling them that you accept them. I had always thought that only when I cleaned up my act would I be acceptable to others. I had often tried to cleanse myself, but never succeeded. Having failed to become acceptable to myself I thought I would never be acceptable to others. Their acceptance of me, in the face of my inability to accept myself, proved me wrong. I do not have to be a particular way to receive others' acceptance. All I have to be is fully who I am, unacceptable and all.

My return from the woods that dawn became a symbol. I had to run away from myself to discover how to come back to my Self. My failed attempt to escape helped me accept my captivity. When I was prepared to be imprisoned by the person I am, I found a liberation coming from some place in me I never knew existed.

## *Latania: Reaping with Songs of Joy*

My demeanor was too unorthodox for many of my classmates. They had told me that my hair was too wild, that they did not like my use of black language, that I would never fit in a white world. But at the Farm, I was a full-blown conservative. That was not my plan. It just happened.

I showed up primed to be an Elite. But just in case I was an Out I arrived wearing several panties, two pairs of sweats, a thermal T-shirt, a sweatshirt, and a wool sweater. I never imagined I might be a Middle. Upon learning this I felt like a second-class citizen, because others were telling me who I was and what was expected of me. I felt sorry for myself. Then the Outs arrived and I discovered how deprived I could have been. I decided to enjoy the privileges given to the Middles.

I resolved to live the good life. The Outs' plight was their problem! It was not my business whether they got food or had a place to sleep. The Elites could deal with that. I had decent meals and a nice bed. I thought I should care about how the Outs fared, but I really didn't. My only concern was how to hang on to my privileges. The Elites demanded we work, but I refused. I was willing for the Middle men to do domestic and farm chores, but not the Middle women; however, we wanted to be the beneficiaries of the work the men did. Of course our position upset the men, but who cared? It couldn't hurt these men to do a few menial tasks.

It was boring to be invested only in preserving our privileges, but I felt too apathetic to be concerned. We had been manipulated into being an irrelevant force. Having the good life stopped us from siding with any possible rebellion. But the Elites had been very cunning: if the Outs did revolt, it would be the Middles who lost their meals and their beds. That Elite trick made us into staunch allies of the status quo.

I was indifferent about the "one person, one vote" campaign of the Middle men. I was willing to just go with the flow. Later I was very troubled by this, especially as I watched the Outs eat their first decent meal after days of only peanut butter sandwiches. I realized then how much my privileges had anaesthetized me to the Outs' plight. How strange to have been a poverty-stricken person in the past and be so unaffected by the deprivation of these Outs!

During the review I got disturbed by how disengaged I had been. I did not know why this had happened. I was jealous of others who were getting insights that would change their lives, while I sat there, seemingly dead. I had expected so much from the Farm and had got so little. I knew that we got what we sowed. My indifference meant I was reaping nothing. I got down on myself. But I was too disengaged to do anything useful.

Then an Out said to me, "Why fight it, Latania? Go with it. Perhaps you will find out what you need to learn if you become more disengaged." That was the advice I needed. Soon I saw that I had taken flight into my expectations. Having high expectations and then failing to reach them was my way of fleeing from the actual experience I was having.

I let go of all expectations and withdrew even deeper into my self. I had to fight the idea that I had failed. Only when everything was completely still in me, when I was detached from everyone, did I see what I had been missing. I had been hooked on the idea that the important revelations in life come with a big bang. It was the parting of the Red Sea that convinced those traveling with Moses that it was God who was orchestrating their escape from slavery in Egypt. It was Saul's encounter with a blinding light on the Damascus road that prompted him to listen to the Voice suggesting a different plan for his life. We do not tend to see God in the smaller gestures, in the helping hand, in the quiet acts of kindness.

I started to think about how important it has always been for me to be "at my own place." When I am far away, I long to return. Most people at the Farm were exploring the unfamiliar. Instead of asking what's wrong with me for not doing that, I asked how was it benefiting me to remain located in the familiar. With that insight I went to the most familiar place within me and decided to stay there as long as I could, to explore what the familiar is truly like.

I learned that I have a special place inside me that is my source of rejuvenation. I can't describe it. It is not where I go to cry or to be sad. It is a place of celebration and of new life. It is a place that restores me. All the messages I received from outside told me I had to find or create my own place for my *self* in this world. I believed them. But it turned out that my task was to accept the inner *place* that had already been provided for me. It had always been there. All I had to do was to be willing to live there, in my own special inner place. Then all would be fine.

This was not a place of my own making. It was a gift provided for me at birth. It had been created for me. My people had found it throughout their generations of suffering. Others had cradled it on our collective behalf, and when I was old enough I had been shown how to find it. I had my own special place because my people had found their place. It was not something I could have done on my own. Initially I did not know how to enter it. As loved ones died and I grieved the loss, caring relatives showed me the way into my place. I can't explain it. It is beyond words.

As I described to others this discovery I had made, they said I should celebrate that I had such an inner place to go. They assured me that the only reason they had ventured into foreign lands was to search for the thing I had found within me. As I told them about what this place was like, no one thought I was a misfit any more. They were eager to know me on my terms and to accept me as I am. "How do you get in there?" they asked. My answer surprised even me. "Through my brokenness!" I replied.

## Out of My Depths

By the time I, Kenwyn, had become conscious of myself as a person I felt betwixt and between and wanted solid ground upon which to stand, I felt afraid and wanted to be liberated, I felt a misfit and wanted to belong, I felt crippled by unmet expectations and wanted merely to be, I felt defensive and wanted to dismantle the walls surrounding me, I felt guilty and wanted to be cleansed, I felt closed in by my silence and wanted to burst out, I felt lost and wanted to find the way, I felt broken and in need of repair. I longed for a place that was not this place. I had no words to capture my yearning, so I carried silently the ache that accompanied my dislocation. I was also too restless to stay still, so, at some point, I cannot recall exactly when, I set off on a journey.

At first I was hungry for knowledge about an age-old question, Who am I? Philosophy, psychology, anthropology, and sociology became my passions. The more I read, the more lost I became. Everything was so vast, so magnificent, so interrelated. My academic quest produced emotional paralysis as I pondered if it was possible to grasp life's simultaneous complexity and simplicity!

An alternative beckoned: travel the world. Surely, somewhere in this vastness there was a little corner where I would not feel lost. Visiting unfamiliar territories was glorious. I delighted in the various and colorful ways people lived, such a contrast to my own drabness. Of course, it did not matter what locale I visited or what body of literature I embraced, I did not find calm, for I kept taking my inner restlessness with me.

Failing in my search increased my despair. I gave up hope, until the pain of not looking grew larger than the pain of not finding. A quiet voice from somewhere inside me said, "to understand your predicament look in your own back yard." That proved useful.

My first port of call was my accent. Everywhere I have gone people have asked me a perfectly innocent question, "Where do you come from?" Rarely can anyone guess my nationality given how I sound. That did not trouble me in the international arena, for it was understandable. However, all my days I have been asked this same question, even in the country of my birth, in the place where I grew up. As far back as I can recall, my accent prompted every new acquaintance to quiz me about where I was from. I was asked this so often it led me to believe "I must not belong here," otherwise they would not say this. Each time I faced this, my spirit shrank a little.

I was born to an Australian father and an English mother. I spent the first year of my life in Australia and the second in England. From age two to five I lived in China, and Mandarin became my first language. The only English I ever spoke between the ages of two and five was occasionally in my home and with the Canadian children who lived in our compound in Chengdu, capital of Szechwan province. For the remainder of my childhood and youth I lived in Australia. In my mid-twenties I came to the United States to complete my graduate schooling.

My dilemma was that I never really sounded like an Aussie, but I didn't sound like anything else either, not an Englishman, not an American, not a Welshman. Hence, each time I was asked, "Where are you from?" the juvenile logic of my heart said, "If I do not come from here I must be from somewhere else!" No one thought I came from "here" so I must come from some yet-to-be-discovered "there." Yet every "there" I went, I faced the same question, which convinced me that no *there* existed to claim me as one of its own. This accentuated my feeling that "I must come from *no* where," an awful and awe-filled thought!

Today questions about my accent produce no pain but invite me to celebrate my uniqueness, something I have in common with every person. After all, those who feel they don't belong all belong to the class of people who don't belong, an important lesson the homeless were discovering at the Farm.[13]

I also began to examine an early conclusion I had made about myself: my conviction that I was unlovable. What were its roots? As a small boy in China, Gwai Darn Jung put my brother and me to bed each night. She was a wonderful caretaker, a dear person whom my family trusted fully. I always thought of her as a loving person. Yet something horrible happened each night. She ended our bedtime rituals by telling us Chinese fairy tales; many of them included scary scenes with the dragon. These stories terrified me and gave me nightmares, which I never got to talk about.

When I was five, the communist revolution put us on the opposite side of the world from Gwai Darn Jung and I never sorted this out with her directly. However, as I grew up in Australia I was anguished by these nights I had spent in the grip of terror caused by her dragon stories. Even worse, I was tormented by a two-pronged question. Why would a person who said she loved me scare me as I was going to sleep? And why would my parents let me be terrorized this way by a caretaker? Surely love is more protective than this, I silently mused, a dissonance I resolved by concluding that neither Gwai Darn Jung nor my parents loved me and that when they said they did, they were lying. Of course, my next question was "Why don't they love me?" The logic of the child brought me to a simple answer; "because I am unlovable!"

I had always been troubled by my relationship with my mother. For reasons I never understood, when anything emotional occurred in our family, mother withdrew. Her retreat was extreme and was both emotional and physical. She would often just walk out of the room in response to a child's upset. I grew up assuming this was normal and guessed that adulthood meant having no strong feelings about anything. My father's depressed demeanor reinforced my view that "flat was beautiful."

All this made having any passions problematic. When I was young I was convinced that to have strong feelings about things was wicked. My evidence was that mother bestowed approval only on those who remained calm. How was anyone with my level of emotional volatility ever going to be accepted by her? To win her, I squelched every emotion. What an impossible situation! My mother had some unstated image of what the world had to be like, and I was required to fit into the prescribed mold. I was furious about this but believed my anger was inappropriate, so I suppressed it. I became withdrawn and emotionally inaccessible, a lot like my mum.

Then I started to examine my relationship with my father. I was two years old when I met him for the first time. It occurred on the streets of Bombay. I don't actually remember the event, but the account of our meeting was told often during my boyhood. Dad's repeating the story of our first encounter must have provided some form of therapeutic release for the family, because it was aired often. Yet its telling had a devastating effect on me. This story, I now recognize, was at the core of my trauma as a child.

A little family context is needed. Both my parents had gone to China as missionaries in the early 1930s, my father from Australia, and my mother from England. They met in the late 1930s and were married in Shanghai in 1940. About the time I was conceived they were going to Australia for an extended leave. The whole world was at war and it was dangerous for families to be traveling. They made it to Australia but my dad was immediately drafted for military service. To avoid this fate he returned to China right away, leaving my mother and brother in Australia to await my birth. A year later mother, with two small boys, set off for England to visit her family and to wait until we could safely join my father in China. Somehow we got to England even though the oceans were filled with submarines and destroyers, the navies of both friend and foe.

A year later we left for Asia. Mother and we two boys went by ship to Bombay. There we met up with Dad. We then traveled as a family to central China, where we lived for the next few years, until the communist revolution of 1949, as history ended up determining.

We were always at the dinner table when the tale about the day I met my father was told. Often there were visitors. I hated those times. Feelings would arise in me I could not escape. I was embarrassed. I would grit my teeth with the hope of getting through another telling without disgracing myself. The punch line was packaged as, "what a cute young boy I must have been." Everyone would laugh. Me too! It was the only way I knew how to hide. I wanted to run away.

My father's telling of the story went as follows. It was very hot in Bombay that first day of our relationship. We had been walking a great deal. As a two-year-old I quickly tired and asked my mother to carry me, but she said no. My father offered to pick me up, but I refused to let him. I didn't want to be in the arms of this strange man. I wanted my mother and no one else! I made a scene, behaving so badly that my dad gave me a spanking, right there on the streets of Bombay, on the first day we met! "And then, that night, as I was tucking the boys into bed," my father would say with all the flare of a great storyteller, "Kenwyn looked up at me and said, 'Daddy, tomorrow I'll let you carry me.'" That's when I wanted to run away, for I was not able to deal with all the emotions packed into this story.

As I began to attend to this narrative, I recognized how much of my character as an adult was identifiable when I was two. I have always found it difficult to depend on others, to let anyone carry me when I've been needy. No one would have described me as a trusting person. I was so fiercely independent, others were more likely to view me as a man who had problems with trust. And here, in the beginning of my relationship with my dad, I could see the same things. I had not trusted my father to carry me when he offered. After getting a spanking I capitulated to him. I was the new kid on the block, and I had better start by earning my place in the order of things.

These four themes — where do I come from, my mother's extreme withdrawal, my early nightmares, and my father's spanking — all came forcefully into my awareness as I explored my conviction that I was unlovable. And there lurking in the crevices of my spirit were four companion emotions: a paralyzing terror, extreme uncertainty about the trustworthiness of the world, a seething rage, and a desire to run away.

I was remembering my struggles with these questions while listening to the Farm Outs. Arun had captured perfectly how I felt about my early history during the Outs' trek to the Farm: We are all searching for something, but will we be able to recognize what we desperately want to find when it comes? In my case I had no hope of being "at home" with myself until I shifted my ways of thinking about life.

In my young adulthood I had traveled to many distant lands before I discovered that the journey I had to make was into the uncharted landscape inside me. It was easy to catch a plane to Paris or Bali and revel in the sights, sounds, and smells of exotic places, but these did not satisfy my yearnings. Ultimately I was to learn that these places were no match for the grandeur of the heart, even one as underdeveloped as mine.

Like Arun, I also was caught between two cultures. In an attempt to flee from the constraints of my Australian self, I too had ended up at graduate school in the United States. I enjoyed three very enriching years on this side of the world. Upon arriving in America I tried to acculturate myself, not wanting to be a misfit in this new place. In time I acquired some different lenses, and this gave me a new perspective on my Australian heritage. I was eager to return to my homeland, to reclaim all I had left behind. However, I had internalized so much of this new culture that I had unwittingly become bicultural in a new way: I no longer fully *fit* in either Australia or the United States. Without even knowing it, I had added an American-Australian axis to the East-West dichotomy of my childhood and the British-Colonial dimension of my parentage.

From then on, whether I was in America or Australia, a big part of me yearned to be in the other location. For several years I spent nine months here, three months there, and then reversed it, as I tried to be emotionally in both the United States and Australia, while never living fully in either. The very form of my search to discover why I did not feel at home had made me the creator of the very nomadicism I wanted to escape.

I was also just like Daniel, for I too knew early in life that I would leave my place of birth and seek a new home. Like him I had a glimmer that my departure would be enacting something for my whole family, which I sensed was trapped in some invisible prison from which we all needed to be liberated. I was determined to break out, thinking that if I could get free, my parents and siblings would be released too. That was pure myth, of course, but for me it felt real at the time. My question was whether I, Kenwyn Kingsford Smith, had to be on the road, or was it that a part of my family had to depart and I was the one doing the leaving on behalf of us all? Maybe I was to be the hero, liberating all. Or maybe I was just the goat, the misfit whose departure would unify those left behind because they all shared the same feelings about the part of them that had gone.

There was also the model of my own parents, which I could have been following. Both my mother and father had gone to China from England and Australia respectively in their early twenties and lived there for almost two decades. They had both been searching for something that they found, at least temporarily, a world away. Today, this does not seem unorthodox. However in the 1930s, long before air travel and China's even having a road system, this was adventurous beyond comprehension. Returning home for Christmas or a wedding was out of the question. Mail took months and phones were but a dream in places with no electricity or running water.

At age forty my parents were forced to leave China due to the revolution of 1949, abruptly ending the life they had been creating together. They would have returned were this ever possible, but the doors to China were permanently closed to them. They had lost their home. A quiet depression descended on our family, one that was never discussed.

I also identified strongly with Blair. I had been a runner all my life. In fact my earliest memories were of running. It was early in the morning. My parents had concluded it was too dangerous to stay in China another day. The revolution was breaking all around us, and Westerners were no longer welcome in this land. Getting away was not easy. It was raining. I was told to make a dash for the plane and climb quickly aboard. My little five-year-old legs went as fast as they could. I thought they wanted me not to get wet. It was only when I learned, years later, that the communists tried to shoot down that plane, that I understood the real reason I had been running.

Like Daniel, Arun, Latania, and Blair, I had lived much of my life fleeing from one thing or another. Only when I turned to face my brokenness did anything change.

During our review session Arun said something that opened the door to the celebration of our brokenness, a reality that Latania and her people understood. "I am no longer afraid of being afraid. I have stared my fears in the face and know that I am truly terrified. I will not deny my fears any longer. I am completely lost in life and I have no idea what I am doing in this world. However, I refuse to act as if I do when I don't. I've always lacked the courage to say honestly what I think, to state the unspeakable. No more. I will say what is in my heart and on my mind, for only that way, to my own self can I be true. I will be silent when I would normally speak, and I will force myself to speak when I usually silence myself."

That kind of self-acceptance was a good start for the lost souls at the Farm.

> *Thou hast traced my journey and my resting places,*
> *and art familiar with all my paths.*
>
> Psalm 139:3

# Chapter 6

# Steal a Way Home

The Outs at Beacon Hill were furious that the Elites and Middles tried to strip them of their identity. They were convinced that the haves were driven only by their self-interests and were not concerned about the well-being of the have-nots. The Elites and Middles took this action because they wanted to create a place were everyone would feel at home. Clearly, it didn't work. When the Outs arrived at Beacon Hill they began to thieve with impunity. This upset the haves, who failed to see the behavior of the have-nots as a mirror of their own. The Elites and Middles tried to snatch from the Outs the freedom to revolt, and the Outs stole to ensure they remained masters of their own fate. Everyone became thieves at Beacon Hill, even though the espoused value of that society's planners was to build a world were there was no need to steal a thing.

The dynamics at the Farm were very different. The Outs elected to see themselves as surrounded by abundance, and hence the very concept of thieving never entered their consciousness. Had anyone tried to steal from them, they would have treated it as irrelevant, for thieving is possible only in a world of scarcity. One cannot steal oxygen from another when air is freely available to all; were it scarce, one person's breathing might mean another went without, and there could well be battles over who was entitled to the air and who was not. Some might even look for a tablet of stone to see if it was recorded in antiquity that one had a stronger claim to oxygen than another. Some might even claim that God is invested in their getting more breath than their adversary. Mercifully, unless the environment becomes completely polluted, air is not in short supply.

Stealing is a common method used to deal with the anguish created by the clash between our suffering and creative selves. While it is rarely discussed in these terms, the stealing we all do is full of rich insights. It contains data about how not to steal; it can also show us that the whole landscape is awash with abundance if only we would stop looking at it in scarcity terms.

I am grateful to three white women at the Farm for being willing to look at their actions using the stealing lens. These women, two Outs and one Elite, forthrightly examined how they stole others' emotions to avoid having to deal with their own. That unearthing led them to find some of the many emotional gifts freely available to all and left them no longer needing to steal.

I am cautious, as a white man, to use women's experience to exemplify this theme of emotional theft. It would be easy, but wrong, to characterize this as a female foible, for men do this constantly, even though we rarely acknowledge it. Hence, in addition to exploring the stories of these women, I use the frame of stealing to examine a problematic part of my own history. I feel able to explore this topic here because of the courage of Trisha, Christine, and Juliet.

## *Trisha: Setting Me upon a Rock*

I liked the changes being an Out produced in me. In the past I'd been quiet in groups. I tried not to be, but the harder I worked at it the more I became what I resisted. I knew I muzzled myself, but I never knew how a group silenced me. At the Lab, rather than combat my condition, I accepted it. That freed my energies and gave me so much vitality I had a big impact in the Out group and the whole community.

My moment of awakening came early. Something one of the domineering men did upset me, and I went right at him. Others were startled to see quiet and accommodating Trisha pushing this big guy around. I was angry and told him I was directing my rage at him because of the hostility he had toward women, some of which he sprayed on me. He was stunned and did not understand. I said, "What upsets me most is you don't listen when I speak. I think that's because I am a woman! You treat my ideas as irrelevant. But when a man says the same thing, you get excited and support him. That's unacceptable to me. On the other hand, with you I must fight to get heard. That's good for me. I'm determined to have you listen when I speak. Getting men to listen when I speak is a skill I need. And I'm going to practice it on you."

He shocked me by responding truthfully. "I am so out of it I usually don't bother listening to you, Trisha. However, it is not just you. I don't listen to anyone. I am detached from everything all the time. I have no idea why. If this has something to do with my sexism, I am not conscious of it." I never imagined that men might ignore me because I was a woman. I assumed others did not listen because my thoughts were no good. I got firm with this guy: "Well, I think it is your sexism, and there's no reason for women to tolerate it. I want you to stop treating us this way. We are going to confront all forms of sexism in our Out group, whether you like it or not." To my surprise, others were eager to do this too, the men as well. Soon we were all saying things like, "How is our thinking on this issue influenced by our maleness or our femaleness?" It was so refreshing.

If an Out man did not listen to me, I went after him with a vengeance. As I did this I recognized how my family of origin influenced my behavior. There was so much conflict in my house, I had to scream to be heard. It was not a physically abusive place, but the emotional violence was fierce. I hated the fights. I retreated to my room and locked my door when they occurred. I always thought I must raise my voice and scream to be heard, but at the Farm I noted that I generally waited until there was chaos before I tried to speak. This was an old pattern. When I was young I delayed saying what was on my mind until the family was in disarray. Only then did I speak. To avoid being ignored, I yelled. I resented my family for this. It felt good to blame them. Meanwhile, I took no responsibility for what I was doing. I played out this same pattern in the Outs until flashbacks from my childhood came. Then a lot of repressed memories returned, showing me how my self-silencing and the silencing of me by groups had been working in tandem.

I was excited to discover I could alter this by just changing *me*. I didn't have to change everyone else. I always thought that to stop feeling helpless I had to change others. Life with the Outs taught me that by changing how I acted, the part of the world most relevant to me altered automatically. I began forcing others to listen to me. I decided to say what was on my mind and in my heart, no matter what. If someone did not like it, they could tell me, but I would no longer be quiet just to avoid being ignored. The Outs welcomed my voice when it was strong and were excited to follow my lead when I was filled with the convictions that came from within. That was scary to begin with, but I grew to like it.

At the Farm I examined something about myself that had always troubled me: I always identified strongly with the pain of others but rarely accessed my own. During one of my many walks alone I stumbled on a frozen pond. I stared at it for a long time. It seemed like a metaphor. Inside me was a lot of tumult but on the outside I was like a frozen being. Looking at the pond I recognized how much I tuned into other's feelings, but rarely tapped my own. I asked myself, "Do I soak up other people's pain to dull my own or because it is easier to deal with their feelings than mine? Do I feed off other's angst to make myself feel like a whole person?" I soon realized I could not unravel what was going on so I threw caution to the wind. This cracked open my icy exterior and let out some of what was inside me. My emotions emerged slowly at first, but after a couple of days they came fast and furious.

Someone asked, "Trisha, do you live off others' feelings to avoid having an emotional life of your own? Do you like having a second-hand life?" That was the shove I needed. I stopped doing it right there and then! I began to tune into my own feelings first and express them instead of waiting for other's emotions to come out and grafting myself onto them. Soon the barriers tumbled down, and I was like a young chick being born. I grew at a pace even I could notice. I started taking initiatives and, to my delight, others followed my lead.

I had a wonderful time with the Outs. The character of our belonging was special. I don't mean we got along. *We truly belonged* to one another, were powerfully connected to each other. Part way through I realized that I had never let myself be part of anything before. I was too much of a loner. I'd seen how others erected walls to prevent themselves from belonging, but I'd never noticed that I did the same thing.

My attachments with the Outs showed me how detached I'd been in life. Over recent years I had made very few friends. Instead of joining with the people who were around me, I had relied on a small circle from my past. However, those old friends were far away and did not meet my current needs. The Outs taught me how to embrace the people nearby as friends. After the Lab, others reached out to me continuously. They kept encouraging me to ask them for help rather than going it alone. No longer was I emotionally isolated. Others were caring for me and about me. I was amazed by how many people wanted to connect with me when I opened myself to them. And the more connected I was to others the more connected I was to myself. I always believed that if I gave away too much of myself, there would not be enough left for me, an old tape that played endlessly in my brain. No more. That tape was erased. A new one emerged to take its place: the more I genuinely give of myself to others the more authenticity I have for myself.

## Christine: Love That Endures

I once thought of myself as a sensitive person who was very empathic. I felt others' emotions so keenly I often wept their tears, vented their rage, expressed their joy. And I congratulated myself for being so attuned to them. Life with the Outs showed me that I regularly inserted myself into situations where I did not belong, grafted my emotional self onto others, had their feelings on their behalf, while simultaneously feeding some unknown monster inside me with others' pain, anger, or happiness.

I saw that in the past I often intervened when people were engaged in a verbal battle. Instead of letting them sort it out I would rush into the middle of it, even when it had nothing to do with me. I would eventually be caught in the verbal crossfire, get myself hurt, and burst into tears. All action would cease;

everyone would turn to me and ask why I was upset. I would tell them about how much pain I felt while the combatants were slugging it out, and the fight would stop, at least temporarily. Then I would privately applaud myself for ending the battle before it got out of control and be puzzled about why it took my being hurt to have the fight stop. I was doing no one a service by behaving this way. But until my classmates pointed this out to me, I never saw how much I interfered in others' relationships; it seems that I would never allow people to connect with one another without my being in the middle of it.

When the Outs forcefully told me they did not want the kind of empathy I offered and grilled me on why I inserted myself in others' battles, or why I was crying, or why I was trying to control events, my response was that I was highly identified with their emotions. This was true at one level; but this truth was so partial, at another level it was false. The reality was that having the attention turn to me gratified something inside me.

It took a while to crystallize, but I eventually saw that I did it to hide from my own emotions. By draining off the pain, joy, frustrations, or anger of others and experiencing these emotions on their behalf, I masked my own feelings. My empathizing with others was my way of escaping from my emotions. What a revelation! With force the Outs told me, "It's hard enough trying to grab hold of our emotions, especially the ones we disown, without having you hitching your wagon to them. It's oppressive. You think it is a lifeline, but it's an albatross. Express, explore, examine your emotions to your heart's content, but do not piggyback them on the rest of us. Let each of us deal with our own struggles without your unwanted interference." This was the catalyst for change I needed.

Trisha had strong and impervious boundaries. I was the opposite. I was like an emotional sponge. But we had one thing in common: we both felt trapped by outmoded gender dynamics. I did not have to fight to be heard, as did Trisha. My tears and emotional volatility provoked others to ask what was going on for me. By presenting myself as weak I got the attention I craved.

In the Out shelter we put a lot of energy into exploring the differences between male and female reactions to things and worked hard to alter those historical patterns that have messed up male-female relationships. Eventually we mastered it and stopped doing male or female routines to get each other to listen. We all just said forcefully what we thought or felt, and each person's assertions were valued even when they were disagreed with. This was unfamiliar for me.

Like others, I left the Farm determined to speak my mind and not filter it for others' consumption. I was nervous about where this would lead but decided this would be a better path than the one I'd been on. First, it led me to reexamine my relationship with the Catholic Church. Oh, how I have felt wounded by the sexism in my church. When I was young I thought it was my calling to be a nun. But by mid-adolescence I couldn't tolerate the church's refusal to let women be full-fledged ministers. I could not imagine a life separate from the church, but I would no longer go along with the male domination that blocked me from what I thought was my destiny, being a cleric. I grew away from God and blamed the church. In time I drifted toward Protestantism. I even considered preparing to become an Episcopalian minister but....

Another problem for me was my relationship with men. While I had the normal romantic partners during my adolescence, as an adult it grew harder and harder to imagine finding a man I would consider marrying. At a certain point I would back off from a potential relationship. I did not want to admit why, but after the Farm I decided I would avoid it no longer.

I chose to confront my childhood history of sexual abuse at the hands of my stepfather. My anger at men came from this. I hated him for the abuse and for making me feel guilty for what was not my fault. When I added this to the church's position on women I felt at a loss.

The Outs proved to be my salvation. They forced me to get clear about my own emotions and to keep them untangled from others' feelings. Thanks to Trisha, I was with a group that explored the impact of sexism on our interactions with one another. Being an Out opened me to the changes my spirit craved.

Two years after being at the Farm I had learned how to be at home with myself. Old patterns that had served me poorly over the years were gone. I stopped affixing myself to others' emotions and found an inner rudder. Also, I fell in love and got married. Yes, in the Catholic Church. Having made peace with myself, I was able to accept the flaws in others, even the church.

## Juliet: Waking the Echoes

I was an Elite with access to the resources, yet most of the time I felt powerless. It was odd! Trisha, as an Out, felt extremely powerful, while as an Elite, I felt perpetually weak.

We haves put so much energy into dealing with the homeless issue but had no conception of what their problems actually were. Only during the review period, when we learned how to listen to the have-nots on their terms, did we understand. When we connected with them, we were surprised to find that we Elites were the ones who felt least at home in the world we had created.

It was hard to take in what life had been like for the Outs. I felt responsible for them, had tried to save them and to make them more like us. The only thing I wanted to hear was they were grateful for all we did for them. Being forced to listen to them talk about the gems hidden in their suffering was too much for me. I felt the purpose of my existence as an Elite had been for naught.

In time, I accepted that the Outs had made good use of their experiences as the have-nots, stopped blaming myself for all that had happened, and began looking at my own life through the same lens they had used. This brought a rush of emotion and many startling lessons as I looked at where my images of "home" had come from.

The emotions I had felt most often in life were anger, guilt, deception, and betrayal. Before the Farm I had no idea why I had always reacted tempestuously to things that did not disturb others at all. Listening to the Outs pried open some long-locked memories. Surfacing were some dark family secrets. I had hidden from myself the reality that I had been physically abused as a child. While somewhere in me I must have known this, it had been deeply repressed. The abuser was my father, although he was clearly passing on the abuse he'd received.

My father had been raised by a stone-like, unaccepting man for whom he worked until his early thirties. Dad was perpetually angry with his father but was unable to express it to him directly. He found an alternative outlet: me. With an uncontrolled rage he beat me. I thought this was because I was bad, but the reality was he used me as his emotional garbage dump. Dad unleashed on me the displaced anger he felt toward his father. At the time I was too young to fight back. It continued for years and only ended when he quit working for his father and moved far away.

My mother turned a blind eye to this abuse. She was a young, inexperienced, terrified, and lonely woman, with a workaholic husband and controlling in-laws. She grew up in an alcoholic family with harsh rules and strict consequences attached to every violation. She had survived by making herself an expert on all the nuances of her family's rules. In our family she replicated this rule-dominated and punishment-filled environment. As a girl I was afraid I would violate a family rule and be punished. To avoid this I was obedient and made sure to be seen as good. I had an overdeveloped conscience and felt guilty even thinking about doing something outlawed. Like my mother and father before me, I was very angry with my parents, but refused to direct it at them.

Instead, I created two outlets. One was straightforward but problematic. I redirected my anger at myself. The other was more complex. Instead of expressing the emotions I felt, I tried to dilute them. I ran around taking in as many emotions from other people as I possibly could, hoping to dampen my own pain. I did this by being best friends with anyone who was wounded. I offered them comfort and found that soothing others' pain provided me with solace. I also assumed that if I relieved others' anguish enough, the world would be kinder to me.

Taking in others' pain fueled something in me that was destructive. My inner pain was like a monster that had to be constantly fed. The only thing that would satisfy it was more pain. What enabled this monster to stay alive was the pain I sucked out of my encounters with others. I was like a parasite, feeding off the pain of others to satisfy something in myself. This had always been unconscious, and before going to the Farm I'd have been devastated if anyone had suggested my kindness to others was self-serving. The other Lab participants helped me acknowledge these truths about myself and not to feel bad about them. Like Trisha and Christine, I had become sophisticated at stealing others' emotions to satisfy some hidden need of my own.

I had to stop siphoning off the pain of other people. It robbed them of the chance to work out their anguish in their own way. Yet where was I to start? To change I had to cease running from my own pain, to admit how awful it was growing up in my family, and to acknowledge how angry I felt toward my parents. Curiously, by just acknowledging this I felt better.

Soon after leaving the Farm I called my mom to wish her happy birthday. That's when many things got clear. I called her only because I felt obliged; she was the last person in the world I wanted to talk to. A phone conversation with her always left me empty. She was skilled at stealing my emotions too. Not this time, though! Something new entered our relationship that day. Rather than blurt out all my thoughts and feelings as I usually did in the hope of getting something from her, I remained contained. I cautiously told her only a small amount about the Lab and waited to gauge her reaction before proceeding. Her response was helpful. She picked up on the different sense of self I was conveying and used this opportunity to talk with me in a way she had not done before. For the first time she told me her feelings about a longstanding family secret: her own father's alcoholism and her joy over his recent success in remaining sober.

We talked as we never had before. As we ended she said, "I had not felt happy about grandpa's sobriety until this conversation. Tonight I sensed your strength. That helped me tell you things I had locked away. You've been very comforting. Thank you." For the first time following a chat with my mom, I felt full rather than empty. Of course, I was no longer denying my emptiness, and that helped me bring my newfound wholeness to my relationship with her.

My family had been disintegrating for a long time. For years I tried to stop it from falling apart, but it was beyond repair and my efforts achieved nothing. Some years back my mom lost interest in my dad, which devastated him. For two decades, she had been his only admirer. Then she began dating my ex-boyfriend. That was so perverse. Actually it was sick. She'd call me to talk about the ups and downs of her love life with my ex, seeking my counsel on her turbulent romantic life. She never considered how this might affect me. Worse still, I allowed her to treat me this way! Meanwhile, I became the main social support for my dad, who would dump on me his grief over losing his wife, punctuating his tales of woe with stories of life with his new squeeze.

Upon leaving the Farm I stopped having any expectations of my family. Being selfless with them encouraged them to exploit me. To survive with my family I had to be tough. So I abandoned my pledge to never hurt anyone's feelings, a decision that resulted from hating to be hurt myself. My attempts to avoid pain had made it so I was constantly being harmed. That had to end. Henceforth I would advocate only my own needs and encourage others to care for themselves. It was hard to make these changes but easier than continuing with how things were.

I soon found that I liked the person I'd become and saw that I had not only survived the pain produced by my family struggles but become a stronger person because of them. That was the Outs' big discovery: adversity can be a great teacher for those open to the lessons it offers.

## Anguish in the Soul

Juliet, Trisha, and Christine felt just as lost as Arun, Blair, Latania, and Daniel. But they had additional burdens. Programmed to expect rejection, they knew how emotionally taxing it was to look for acceptance in places where they were misfits. They were also women with histories of abuse in a male-dominated world.

During the review session these three women participated in difficult conversations about how we are all thieves. We were not speaking of shoplifting or embezzlement, but a more subtle form of robbery, namely, taking others' emotions away from them to satisfy needs of our own. Initially the term "stealing" seemed too harsh to apply to our behavior. Was there not a gentler word? However, we chose to speak of it as thieving so we could see how all-pervasive an aspect it is in how we operate. Society designates certain thefts as criminal and incarcerates people for these acts, yet many thefts, which are far more damaging, are treated as legitimate.

Every time we have an evening meal and a telemarketer calls pushing an unwanted product, isn't that intruder stealing from our precious family time? Every time we turn on the late news to catch the sports scores or the weather and are pounded by a litany of all those killed by fire, sniper, or accident since we arrived home, is not some of the tranquility needed for restful sleep stolen from us? Every time a company downsizes and thousands are laid off while shareholders' and executives' assets increase dramatically, are we not witnessing something akin to the Great Train Robbery?

Powerful changes occurred in Christine, Trisha, and Juliet when they ceased to be part-time thieves of others' emotions and became full-time curators of their own. Each of them had been wounded early in life and had feelings anyone would wish to jettison. But importing others' feelings did not displace their own unwanted ones. And undesirable emotions did not get diluted when counteracting passions were brought in.

•

One cold and damp winter, I was accused of being a thief. His indictment was straightforward: "Kenwyn, you had been stealing her emotions, and she was smart enough not to let you do it anymore." These were the words of a caring but brutally honest therapist as we explored why my first marriage ended.

We met during our teens and got married in our early twenties. We were both emotionally young and knew little about how to be in an authentic relationship. While we had the normal ups and downs, given my limited consciousness I felt the first five years of our married life were great. Then it was suddenly over. Not until it ended did I realize how doomed our relationship had been.

The angry exchanges we fell into convinced me she never loved me, and, given my fears about whether I was loveable,

I was emotionally paralyzed for many months. Years later I recognized the problem was not the nature of her loving, but that I did not know how to receive love. Our struggles threw me into an abyss that was so engulfing, I thought I might remain in this dark place for the rest of my days. For the longest time I did nothing but cry. It was the only way I knew how to express what was in my heart. By the time my tears temporarily let up she and I were strangers, our words communicating nothing. We saw no option but to deal with our broken selves without each other.

When she came into my life I felt full, but her departure had left me feeling empty. I accused her of stealing something from me that I imagined I would never regain, my fullness. I was right that I was never to feel full again. It was not true that she had taken my fullness away. What had vanished with her absence was the elaborate method I used to hide myself from my own emptiness, that hollow, cavernous, shadowy side of me. I was to discover that my emptiness had always been a big part of me, but until this crisis I was not aware it even existed. I had hidden from this by filling myself with her. In the language of the Farm, I had tried to steal her heart to fill the part of mine that felt incomplete.

That was why the therapist's statement about my being a thief was so apt. It hurt terribly, but it opened a crack in my inner wall sufficient for me to take a peek at that void, first from a safe distance and then step-by-step, with more closeness. What I saw inside me was an empty cavern filled with endless darkness. Emblazoned above the portal to my hollowness were the same words that had been with me since the beginning: "You Are Unloveable!"

Ever so slowly I concluded, "If this is me, I had better get to know my self." For a while I made a new error as problematic as the old one, only its opposite. I assumed there was nothing inside me but empty places. That was not true. My emptiness was just a part of me. I wasn't all full *or* all empty. I was both full *and* empty. That discovery was still a long way off, however.

For a time, nothing was more important to me than dealing with this problem of my lovability. I searched hard to find the cause, assuming that if I could isolate the source I could eradicate it. That achieved nothing! I worked to make myself over, to elevate the flat planes and smooth out the craggy edges, to become acceptable to both friends and strangers. That achieved even less! I tried to fill myself with others' love, especially the kind that came packaged with no price tag and no demand for repayment. This anesthetized me a bit, but was no cure.

My therapist asked me, "How does a person who's convinced he's unlovable function?" Without thinking, I blurted out, "I have to earn the love I need; and if that fails I must steal it!"

I had no idea about how to receive love as an unconditional gift. When others gave me love I rejected it because it did not fit my definition. What did I think love was? I don't know. I was too caught up in how to get "it," to work out what "it" was that I wanted to get. I had many maneuvers to control others' behavior, but if anyone fell for my orchestrations I ceased to respect them, thereby making their gifts of love meaningless. I had yet to learn how to love myself. The more I labored to have people love me, the more unlovable I became to myself, making my quest futile.

Fortunately, I got depleted. In despair I gave up expecting I could make myself loveable. This proved to be the medicine I needed. Letting go of my machinations moved me away from looking for the cause of all that troubled me and pushed me into being whatever I was. Once I accepted my fears, I ceased to be afraid of being afraid. I was no longer trying to convince myself I was anything other than a lost soul. And I was neither being silenced by nor was I trying to silence my demons. In fact I was arguing vigorously with inner voices I had never listened to before and refusing to take paths that I saw led nowhere. I was learning that fear could be quite an energizer.

A few years later my older brother and I were planning a trip to China. Our father was soon to be seventy-five, and we wanted to celebrate by taking him back to where he had spent the first two decades of his adult life and to visit the scenes of our own childhood. It had been thirty-five years since our narrow escape as the communist revolution erupted all around us.

Planning for this journey was not simple. Dad had Parkinson's disease. He felt shaky about his health most of the time and vacillated constantly about the wisdom of this trip. There was another huge complication. Dad had been one of the men hunted by the communists. He was *to be shot on sight!* I had known this fact for twenty years. My dad had never spoken of it. But two Canadians, both physicians and great friends of my parents from China, visited Australia when I was at the university. I had been their chauffeur for a couple of weeks. Because they were doctors and the Chinese needed their medical expertise they had been allowed to stay for another year after the revolution. So they knew things my father did not and filled in many gaps for me. The bottom line was the communists acted as if my dad was a CIA agent. Whether or not he was working for the CIA, a fact I still had not discerned at the time we were trying to take him to China, I was eager to know if we would be placing him at risk by going to a place where he had once been viewed as an enemy.

I did all the necessary diplomatic investigations to find out if his name had been cleared. I discovered that he had remained on the wanted list for over two decades, through the revolution Mao called the Great Leap Forward in 1958, and well beyond the so-called Cultural Revolution of the 1960s. Only in the 1970s was he taken off the rolls of the hunted. By then China had moved on from wanting to redress the errors of the pre-communist era, was trying to build new relationships with the rest of the world, and had decided that hanging on to old animosities of this kind was pointless. I was satisfied we could visit China safely.

So off to China we went, my brother, our aged father, and I. What surprises there were in store for us! First, I discovered that my dad had lost his heart to China. There, on the streets of Kung Ming, Xian, and Chengdu, he was a different person than the one I had known. In Australia, my dad seemed so small, a man shrunken by destiny. However, speaking fluent Mandarin with the Chinese some thirty-five years after he had been expelled from this land, I witnessed a character with such largesse he was hardly recognizable. In the market place he assembled a crowd who watched curiously as he bartered to reduce the price of an apple from four cents to three. Since this was my dad, the street theater of it all was exciting to witness. I had rarely heard him speak about anything with force, yet alone allow himself to be playful and joyous. In China my father had such intensity, such charisma, such vitality. I wondered where this part of him had been all my growing-up years. I was both happy and sad. When the revolution of 1949 forced him to flee the place where he felt most at home, a big part of his spirit became dormant. However, it had not died.

As soon as we were on Chinese soil I recalled my child-hood nightmares and also my intense hatred of Chinese music. It put my nerves on edge, like a fingernail scratch on a black-board. This made being in China difficult because the music of this culture was everywhere. My Walkman saved me. Mozart, Brahms, Chopin, and their many friends drowned out this local cacophony.

I thought about Gwai Darn Jung's bedtime stories filled with the exploits of the dragon. The dragon is a powerful emblem in Chinese culture, and I knew little about what it conveyed. I was fascinated by dream symbology in general and absorbed all I could of what the Freuds, Jungs, and Joseph Campbells of the world said on this topic. So what did the Chinese dragon mean? It symbolized the emperor's power, capturing the unifying and vitalizing forces of nature, just one level down from what's universally described as God. It was neither good nor bad, but expressed the totality and harmony of inner opposites, like the ultimate Yin and Yang. It was not scary, at least not for the Chinese, just as the Australian Aborigine's totem of the kangaroo frightens no one.

Learning that one fact began a powerful change in me that I celebrate to this day. I quickly recognized that even by age four I had internalized the dragon of the West. In the West the dragon is a devouring creature that emerges from a cavernous abyss to consume us, unless we keep throwing it another maiden upon which to feast. (Now there's a story about sexism worth examining.) In a flash, I understood what had happened to me. I had listened to Gwai Darn Jung's bedtime stories using the Western symbol of the dragon and not the Eastern one. The result? Childhood nights filled with terror.

That realization was magical. I immediately understood that my fears had been a mere accident of clashing cultures and was in no way a statement of my being unlovable to the heart of this

Chinese woman. Gwai Darn Jung had never set out to wound me. She was not one of those "evil communists" I had been told about during my boyhood in Australia, where the political rhetoric of the cold war era claimed that anyone who did not think like we did would kill us if they got half a chance. Her actions had been completely innocent. Even my parents, who had not intervened to protect me, had not been unkind. They had simply failed to understand what was going on in the heart of a lad who lacked the emotional vocabulary to say what had tied his young spirit in knots.

A moment that took my breath away occurred when we returned to the house where we lived. We were in Chengdu, and everything was confusing. Ninety-five percent of the buildings were new and my dad could not get his bearings. Even parts of the river that he used as his coordinates had been relocated. We wondered if we would find any familiar places.

One day we were driving along, and I asked our escort to take an unexpected turn. My brother and my father asked me what I was doing. "We are very close to the house where we once lived," I said. "We're at least two miles away," they argued. "Just indulge me," I replied, as I requested the van driver to stop. I got out and called back to them. "If we go down this alley, we'll find a lane that leads to the old church on the left. There will be a hole in the wall and once we pass through it we'll find our house on the right." I was going on the intuition of a five-year-old, which was out of alignment with my father's and brother's memory. However it turned out my youthful instincts were correct. There sat the old house.

The last night I had spent in that home, three and a half decades earlier, had been panic filled. My memory was of us all frantically packing a few clothes into a bag to prepare for an early dawn departure. Evidently the communists were fast closing in on that city and, as Westerners who were sure to be killed if we did not get out, the pressure was on. I understood that anything I could not carry in my five-year-old arms was to be left behind and I would never see it again. It was survival time. If we could just get out alive we would thank God for the rest of our days.

My father knew he was wanted by the communists and was sure we would all be captured if he tried to leave with us, that we'd be shot without any legal recourse. He wanted to split us up. His plan was to have my mother and us kids leave Chengdu at daybreak, on what was anticipated might be the last flight out before the city fell to the communists. If we could get to Chongping the chances were high we could catch a plane to Hong Kong, where we would wait until we could board a ship going to Australia. Of course, the planes were minuscule in those days. The largest ones in China were old military DC-3s, which could carry only a handful of passengers.

Dad decided he would head off for the hills to the West. He knew this terrain well and believed he could make it, by foot, to Moscow via Mongolia and Siberia. When he reached safety he would figure out how to get to a major European port where he could get passage to Australia. This meant our family would be separated for months. If something went wrong and the planned reunion failed to occur, the survivors might never know what happened to whomever was lost. Mother would not stand for such a scheme. That evening she and my dad had the worst fight of their marriage. She had been through too much. Two years of marital separation during the last part of World War II while raising two small boys alone, and now this! My sister was but a few weeks old, her birth having been induced early to avoid having to flee during the last days of a pregnancy. Mother's desperate outburst ended the argument: "No! We all leave together! We escape together or we die together!"

Silence captured the rest of that evening. Brave souls and innocent children steeled themselves for an unknown journey ahead. Oh, how I have known that silence. The same hush that attended our packing that night punctuated our family life in Australia whenever anger, fear, or uncertainty appeared. That dark night in China gave birth to a piece of family folklore that never faded: impossible emotions are best dealt with by silence. There was no bedtime story that night and our restless sleep was not the result of clashing symbols of the dragon, for our demons had become real. This might be the last time we went to sleep in this life.

Now, there I was standing with my older brother, peering at the house we had lived in all those years ago. We were silent. This time our stillness was not the product of fear but emerged from a sense of the sacred. Our worst fears, born on that night back in 1949, had never materialized. We were alive. However, the effects of those fears had never died. As a family we had made fear our silent companion, an unnamed guest at every meal time, an unseen comrade in every skirmish, an unacknowledged stranger in every intimate moment. Now in the quiet, all that had blessed us and all that had cursed us over the years rushed before my eyes.

I chose this moment to tell my brother about my childhood nightmares and my hatred of Chinese music. We had never spoken of this. The silence of our last night in China had prevented many a conversation. I was curious about his experience. He had listened to the same bedtime stories and had been surrounded by the same music. Had the dragon also terrorized him? Did he hate their music too? His answer was no to both questions. Being a little older he already knew the meaning of the dragon and had not been captive to the same emotional maze as I. However, he did offer me some invaluable insight.

"I think I know why you hate Chinese music," he said.

I was all ears.

He pointed to the screened porch in front of us. "Do you remember we slept out there in the hot summer months?"

I did.

"And do you remember that across the lane there was always a group of street musicians playing a motley assortment of instruments as we went to bed?"

I did not recall the musicians.

"Well, my guess is that somehow your nightmares and your fear of the dragon got linked to that music you heard as you slept."

As my brother made this connection, something in me snapped. It was almost a physical sensation. It was as if a stack of cans piled up on top of each other in a supermarket came crashing down and lay at my feet in a rubble. Except these cans did not hold baked beans or pear slices, but long-held thoughts. Suddenly the whole structure of my thinking about my childhood changed.

Some Chinese music was playing in the background at that time. Instantaneously, my feeling about the indigenous music of this ancient land switched from extreme hatred to intense affection. That day Chinese music began to nourish a part of my spirit nothing else could reach. And with great certainty I realized that Gwai Darn Jung had really loved me, that my terror had been an accident.

Many things changed for me upon my return to China. Visiting the location of my childhood traumas opened up a doorway to my inner home that had always been closed. The turning point was finding that this soil was real. The house in which we had lived actually existed. My memories were not a figment of an overactive imagination. I had survived. I was alive. I even felt that if I were to live out the rest of my days with these people who had once wanted to kill my family and me, I would be happy. I could easily find a way to live in China. Most important, I was no longer afraid to examine anything that tormented me.

There was a night when I was totally confused and on the brink of no return. I was dangling on an emotional precipice I had been on numerous times, but I had not been bold enough to go to the edge and look at what was beyond. That night my caution vanished and I went to the border. There I saw the missing pieces of my inner jigsaw puzzle: I was completely full and completely empty, my fullness and my emptiness being each other's complement. I had been empty all these years because I was so full, and vice versa. No longer did I need to steal anything to make me whole.

No one had ever caused me to be empty, nor had anyone made me full. The end of my first marriage had crushed me but also introduced me to my empty and my dark self, what we have come to refer to as the shadow self. It exited me from my personal fiction and ushered me into a life that was real. It made my emotional work straightforward: if I was to know my self I had to embrace my shadow as well as my luminescence, and to keep them connected.

The sacred literatures contain many stories about being in the wilderness and finding God, or more accurately being found by God. Often we think of this wilderness as the one provided by nature and, in our search for God, we go to places where we are enveloped by the beauty of the mountains, the depth of the fjords, the force of the arid, and the strength of the gushing waters. This period of my life taught me that there is also an internal wilderness filled with potency and beauty where one can go to be spiritually fed. We all become more fully who we are when we embrace the inner opposites that pulsate both within us and around us.

*My heart shall rejoice,*
*for Thou hast set me free.*
Psalm 13:5

## Chapter 7

# *Overcoming Emotional Starvation*

In the course of a lifetime everyone experiences periods of emotional undernourishment. We cry out, like newborns, screaming out our angst about being hungry. Sometimes our world hears and offers us sustenance. Sometimes it ignores us. Sometimes it force-feeds us a tasty morsel with no substance. Sometimes it offers a sedative to stop our yelping. Being emotionally underfed tells us that we are not taking in what we need, that it is time to absorb a different set of the feelings floating around in our worlds. Since we are always evolving, our emotional intake needs continual modification or we get depleted.

At the root of emotional malnutrition are *projection* and *introjection,* two psychological dynamics that everyone uses all the time. These processes are most visible when they go awry and surface as "isms" such as racism, imperialism, sexism, paternalism, anti-Semitism, expansionism,[14] classism, heterosexism, colonialism, ageism, and crusaderism.[15] These personal dis-eases and social scourges indicate that what is being taken in does not nourish the soul.

"Projection" is defined as mapping inside onto outside.[16] It is one of the most natural things humans do. We notice in others the things we least like about ourselves. Then we get distressed about the flaw in them and refuse to attend to the troublesome part of our self that parallels it. Or we see in others the things we wish we had, envy them for possessing what we lack, and fail to notice that we carry the same attribute in good measure. Meanwhile we complain that they don't share with us what we think we are missing.

"Introjection" is projection's twin. It is defined as mapping outside onto inside.[17] When we introject, we take in another's view of us and make it our own, whether valid for us or not.

If we scratch the surface of prejudice and bigotry we find projection and introjection everywhere. Hence, any attempt to unravel the social ills of "isms" that contaminate others or are located in our own backyard requires us to enter the projective world.

Here we meet four people who examined how overwhelming it can be to suffer from emotional undernourishment and what it takes to overcome emotional starvation. The experiences of Gloria (an African American who was an Elite), Lee Wan (a Chinese American woman who was an Out), Johannes (an Afrikaner from South Africa who was a Middle), Sharon (a Japanese American who was an Elite), and another portion of my own struggle show the all-pervasiveness of projection and introjection. Each was caught in a familiar but rarely recognized dynamic: when one deals with the conflict between the creative and the suffering selves by projecting the unwanted parts of self onto others, a cycle is set off that leaves everyone emotionally starved. These stories also reveal the flip side of this bind: by reclaiming what was once jettisoned, the accepting self becomes empowered and can help the creative and the suffering selves to be each other's complement, feeding off and augmenting each other. This helps to heal the fractured heart.

Occasionally, those upon whom we project the unwanted parts of ourselves do not introject what was dumped in their laps, defend against it, or act as if our spraying on them our disowned attributes was wrong or evil. Instead they hold that projection on our behalf, not becoming what our projections implied, but lovingly retaining our disowned selves until we are ready to reclaim them. When we re-collect what they held in the interim, we get back what we once tried to discard, except it is returned transformed. To be in the presence of those who do not introject our projections but retain them until we can be reunited with them is to be in the midst of a transcendent loving.

These stories show the emotional nourishment that flows from reclaiming one's projections. They also demonstrate that when they are returned packaged in terms of their projections upon us, we do not have to eat the wrappings, or introject their extruded selves. We can peel off their projections on us until we reconnect to the given-away parts of ourselves. As a reciprocal gift we can carry their projections infused into the package until they too are ready to gather them back in.

## Gloria: Sowing in Tears

I was one of the three African American women in this course, Crystal and Latania being the others. Earlier in the semester, I had a disturbing encounter with Latania. Crystal and I were seen as fitting into the white world, but not Latania, who used Southern black colloquialisms when she spoke. She also had the wildest hair-do. At one point she asked, "Why am I ignored by this group while other blacks are listened to?" A gay white man, Dale, explained, "Well, Gloria and Crystal have the skills to operate according to white standards, but your hair, your speech, everything about you indicate that you do not know how to function with whites. Hence, many doors will be closed to you. If you three black women tried to get a job as a secretary in my father's business, Crystal and Gloria would be chosen, but not you, Latania."

Everyone gasped in disgust at what Dale said. It was the first explicit indication of racism in our midst. We tried to defend Latania by attacking Dale. Not Latania, however. She felt Dale had spoken a truth important for her to hear. Dale's statement to Latania upset me, mostly because I did not listen to her either. I, a black woman, ignored her too. I felt guilty about this. And here I was letting Dale take the heat. He was expressing the racism of many of us, me included. I wanted to clear the air with Latania. This was what happened.

The next time she irritated me I threw caution to the wind. "Latania, what you just said got to me, but I was about to ignore you. Then I asked myself if I was upset with you because you are a black woman. I hate that question. It bothers me so much that I always ask it. For the majority, they can say it was an individual's inadequacy, or someone made a mistake, but for me I always go back to whether it's because I'm a black woman. I want to tell you, Latania, that I've been angry at you. We black people carry such a burden. When one of us acts in ways others don't like, this is projected onto all of us. I have wanted to strangle you for the way you speak. Then I stepped back and said my judgments of you are unfair.

"I decided to try to understand you, rather than accuse you of not saying it right. Who set the standards for us? I had internalized white views and was projecting them onto you. I'm angry when that's done to me, but I was doing the same thing to you. Latania, you were silenced by them and by me. Now I want you to say more, and I don't care how you say it!"

Latania responded. "It is hard to think people do not understand me."

I interrupted. "I'm not saying people don't understand you, Latania. I'm saying your way of talking is not acceptable. But now I'm asking whose standards I use when I make this judgment. The language we grew up with that our grandmothers and grandfathers in the South used — cut off words, black language — is just another way to communicate. We treated you as being less important because you spoke this way. That's why we were not hearing you."

It felt good to own up to how I had dumped onto my black sister the same feelings whites throw at me. Latania did not get upset or push me away. She took in what I said, told me how it troubled her, and thanked me for saying what I thought. She accepted me as I was, even though I had not accepted her as she was. What a gift!

At the Farm I was an Elite. We tried to deal with the Outs, but none of us grasped the real issues for them. So I was excited to start the review session. I was afraid, however, that I would be blamed for all that had gone wrong. That never happened. The Outs were not blaming anyone for anything. I was certain the other blacks would be after my scalp, saying, "It's one thing for us to be abused by whites, but you, Gloria, you who know what it's like! How come you treated us like dirt?" But they never said such a thing.

The Outs merely wanted to know what the Elites' experience had been like. Their affection for one another and for us was contagious. As I listened to them during the review session I realized they understood me and what my inner life was like in the everyday world. I saw that others were getting stronger by being honest and speaking from the parts of themselves that felt rejected. I decided to do likewise. This was how I started.

"There are many things that crush black women, but recently I hit a new low. I've been dating Vince, a white man. Interracial relationships are very demanding, but I'm really happy when I am with him. However, I feel torn up inside. The tensions around white and black issues are intolerable. Logic says we should break up, but my feelings for him are too intense. My dad won't accept him. He sees only Vince's whiteness and believes that means trouble. I love and respect my father, and I am sure there is something in what he says, but he refuses to accept the feelings I have for Vince and wants us to break up just because he's white. Dad feels I will wake up when it is too late. He is forcing me to choose between him and Vince. That's an awful bind! I cannot end my relationship with my father nor can I walk away from the man I love. The tension is so unbearable I hate going near my family any more. As a couple, we are not welcome. Even if I go alone I feel I am not allowed to bring my heart into the house, all because of my father.

"Thankfully, my mother and sister see it differently. They want me to be sure I know what I am doing. They see problems ahead but assure me that I have the inner resources to deal with them. They disagree with my dad but won't join my fight with him. We are being torn apart, and I am seen as wrecking my family, so the burden to resolve it is on me. Being in an interracial relationship is so tough, if our families don't support us, how can we survive? The situation is intolerable."

I was sobbing so hard my voice was weak. But I continued. "As I listened to the Outs I saw what is going on for me. I have no place that feels like home, except when I am alone with Vince. But we can't survive in isolation. Our seclusion is killing something in us. It is hard being an African American woman, but I never expected my people to abandon me, let alone become the cause of such alienation for me."

By the time I had finished speaking many of the people listening to me were in tears. I was very upset, but it felt great to state clearly what had been troubling me and to feel that everyone understood. As I soon learned, my struggle stirred a lot of passions in others, for we all had a story about why it was so hard to fully be who we are and to have a sense of belonging in this world. I sat back feeling for the first time in ages that I was in a place where I could be fully me. What a wonderful dimension these Outs brought to our life together.

A few months later, my relationship with Vince ended. This was extremely painful. He, and he alone, decided it was over. He would not discuss it with me. He came to this conclusion privately and one day dumped it in my lap. When he told me I screamed, "Why, why, why!" and sobbed for days. The only thing he said that I could grasp was, "I am not able to love you as fully as you love me. You deserve someone better than me! I just can't go on this way." I started saying crazy things like, "I can learn to love you less if that's how it has to be." It took me a while to accept that he was not prepared to take our relationship any further. My heart was shattered.

## *Lee Wan: Lifting the Load*

The homeless group was exactly the medicine I needed. For the first time ever, I felt personally congruent. I couldn't believe it when Gloria spoke of her plight. She put into words the very things I was feeling but had yet to say aloud, even to myself. When she told us of her father's ultimatum, "Marry a white man and you will no longer be my daughter," my heart almost stopped. My father had said the same thing to me a few weeks earlier.

We came to the United States from Taiwan when I was a teen. I tried to fit in but did not succeed. I spent my adolescence in blond and blue-eyed California. Even though I am Chinese, I dated and hung with the fair-haired crowd. I was unsure about my attractiveness and believed if all my friends were beautiful that would prove I was too. I got over this but then discovered I was asking if I was intelligent enough to be accepted by others. For years I depended on others' reactions to figure out what I was like.

I was out of synch with my family and its antiquated values. This was made excruciatingly clear when my father rebuked me saying, "We have always stressed the importance of marrying a Chinese man, yet you have fallen in love with an Irishman. Nothing good will come of this. End this relationship right away! You cannot expect the support of this family if you marry him."

I had two reactions, both of which I stifled. The first was, "But I love him, so what does one do with feelings that sweep one away like the tides?" Then I thought, "I have needed to break from my family. Maybe marrying Patrick will sever those ties."

Patrick and I had some serious problems, but I was determined to marry him to spite my father. I knew this was foolish, but I was being stubborn. Patrick was also having difficulties. Taking a Chinese bride to Ireland would not be easy. He felt our marriage would not survive in the United States or Ireland and had concluded London was our best option. But my sights were set on New York and the lure of a job in the Big City. The more I wanted New York the more he held out for London, and vice versa. Patrick decided to go to London alone and let me sort out how I would react. He thought a few months on opposite sides of the Atlantic would give us enough distance to determine if we had a future.

I was upset. We had reached an impasse. I did not want to lose Patrick, but I also did not want to validate my father's views about interracial marriages, since his opinions had been a big part of why Patrick felt we could not live in the United States.

This bind left me feeling paralyzed by guilt. Then I went to the Farm. There I learned how I tried to rid myself of guilt by projecting my unwanted feelings onto others and finding someone to blame for all that was wrong. The prime target for my projections had been my parents. I wanted them to approve of me, but they didn't accept my loving Patrick. What were they to do? Lie to me? Say they approved when they didn't? Change their opinion to match what I want? I would never respect them if I could manipulate them that easily. I sought their approval but rejected their thoughts. If they were not honest with me I would hold them in contempt.

My dad's rejection of Patrick was convenient because a part of me did not approve, either. Privately I doubted this relationship would work, but I ignored these feelings and blamed my dad for feeling the same as I did. If I were confident it was right to marry Patrick, I wouldn't care what they thought. But I was unsure. I wanted their backing to relieve my anxiety over whether I was doing the right thing. Then if my marriage failed, they would be partially to blame. Since they refused to consent I blamed them for that also. Either way, they were to blame. I was not ready to let go of Patrick because I was still living out my rebellion against my father. How cruel to use Patrick this way! It would have been best to fight with my dad directly and not put Patrick in the middle.

Once I was clear about the bind I set up with my parents, I looked at how, why, and when I seek backing from others. I'd made Patrick my new approval system. I tried to force my parents out of this role by pushing Patrick into it. I made Patrick into my father figure and then rejected all aspects of him that remind me of my dad. Actually, I did not know Patrick all that well, yet I planned to marry him. Why? Because he was not my dad. Yet he was so like my dad, it was scary. I had yet to discover what he was like as his own person. All I really knew was what my mind had made him into.

Seeing all that I had put onto Patrick and my father showed me that I did the same thing with other people too. In my mind I made people into characters they'd never been. Sadly, though, not only did I dump my unwanted emotions onto others, I also took in unwanted emotions others flung at me, letting virtual strangers define who I was as a person and then resenting them for this.

In the shelter I learned that, not only was it okay to be wrong and to feel bad, it was wholesome. At the Farm I reveled in making mistakes. It brought instantaneous relief. Giving myself permission to be wrong made me carefree and helped lift the dark clouds that had hung around me. In the past when I was wrong I'd always try to prove I was right to bolster my self-esteem. With the Outs my posture was, "What's it matter if I'm wrong? Who cares?" This helped me acknowledge my judgmentalism and see that others were not judging me as I had assumed. I said what I thought, even if I was wrong, thereby discovering what I truly thought and felt rather than what I imagined others thought I should think and feel. I became real to myself. That helped me to hear what others were actually saying instead of just my thoughts about what they were expressing.

To my delight I found new ways of functioning that were not based on guilt, fear, disapproval, or judgmentalism. I stopped thinking my only option was to manipulate others into having the feelings that would alleviate my own. Getting insight about my judgmentalism showed me that I used guilt induction as my main weapon when I fought. It was painful to recognize that Patrick withdrew from me because how I related to him was stifling. It was suffocating me, so it had to be strangling him. For so long I tried to keep him committed to me by making him feel too guilty to leave. The more I worked to bind him to me, the more he withdrew. The more he withdrew, the more I tried to bind him to me. These were to be our marriage bonds!

Sadly, I learned these lessons too late to save my relationship with Patrick, but at least they saved me. I have resolved to no longer make *my home* in any man or in any place, be it London or New York. While all my life I had worked hard to feel whole, the reality is I feel more at peace and more whole when I admit to myself that I am broken.

## Johannes: Finding Refuge in the Shade

I am an Afrikaner. I came to the United States soon after Mandela was released from prison. Since then, my homeland has gone through change after change after change. I've been frightened to return. South Africa is a different place from the one I left.

I enjoyed the pleasures of the Middle life at the Farm, but it was horrible living in such close quarters with a Chinese American, three African Americans, a Mormon, and two Jews — not because of them, but because of me. This much exposure to diversity was exhausting. It was more than I've had in my whole life. Over and over images of my racism smacked me in the face. I could not see around it or through it. It stared right at me every time I opened my eyes.

I knew the Farm would challenge me. Since being in the United States my racism has terrified me. I've hidden from it all my life. But it had come out. It was ugly. I wanted to run away. But there was no escape at the Farm. All the others saw my racism clearly. But they were not scared by it like I was. It was my problem. They had enough burdens of their own. That gave me the room I needed. They also recognized my racism tortured me and I was trying to deal with it, inept as I was.

The Middle group accepted me just as I am. That was unsettling. Here I was rejecting myself. Why weren't they doing this too! Even when I was feeling not okay they treated me as if I was okay. That helped me move faster than if I had been defensive, as I usually am. What kick-started me was how others were plowing, without caution, into unexplored emotions. This gave me the impetus to examine myself. I learned I had never felt good about myself. My own racism and my people's racism had been poisoning me.

My armor got smashed during one of the fights we Middle men had with the women in our group. At one point, a white man said something belittling to Crystal, an African American. She forcefully told him she would not tolerate being treated this way. I was shocked. I had never seen a black woman speak to a white man like that before. I thought Crystal was way out of line. Instinctively I saw the man as the wounded party and sided with him. I had not noticed that he had first offended her and she was objecting. I was so strongly identified with him I acted as if Crystal had attacked me.

After being confronted by Crystal, this man acknowledged he had been cruel in what he said and that her rebuke was appropriate. This sickened me. I had never seen a white man back down to a black woman before, let alone apologize. "White was right" in my world. I always felt black women should accommodate to what was going on, because the white male position was the only reasonable one. This was the first time I'd heard a white man admit he'd behaved in a racist way. What a shock! I always thought only blacks were racist! I had never even considered what might be in a black person's heart. I figured Crystal took a contrary stand just to cast us white males in a domineering light and cast blacks as martyrs. I saw her as crass.

As I opened my eyes and saw Crystal as she was, I was stunned. She was a strong woman with rock-like principles and the courage of her convictions. Her integrity was huge. I was an emotional infant beside her. Crystal was not swayed to a position just to avoid being out of step with others. That was the opposite of me. I never was out of line with the dominant opinion or stood up for what I believed. I'm not sure I even knew what I believed.

During the review she explained how hard it was to sort out what she was responsible for versus what she, as an American of African descent, had to live with in this society. For the first time, I saw the pain of a black woman's experience and recognized that most of it was caused by the actions and insensitivities of people like me. I felt shame and horror.

The crack in my defenses was growing wide, and I was terrified. Earlier someone suggested I did not even see blacks as people. I was shocked and treated this accusation as an insult. But he was right. I had not treated blacks as people. I saw myself as enlightened, but years of indoctrination, South Africa's way of life, and my beliefs had caused me to see them not as people, but merely as blacks. I tried to escape my shame by making myself into the one who had been wronged. Any pain I felt I blamed on the people suffering most from my poison. I wanted to be seen as the one being oppressed, not as the oppressor.

When I learned that Gloria was romantically involved with a white man, my racism hit boiling point. My Afrikaner heritage had drilled into me that mixing the races was degenerate. To make matters worse, I was sexually attracted to Gloria, and that made me uneasy about her. I fought my discomfort by looking for things about her I thought were unacceptable. Once I knew she was romantically involved with a white man, I replaced my feelings of attraction with ones of disgust. Mixed-race dating was unacceptable to me, even though some part of me wanted to experience it. The only person I felt contempt for though was Gloria, not her partner. I held him accountable for nothing. I had never considered whites as responsible for any racial problems.

All these feelings were so overwhelming I could not conceal them. However, the people of color at the Farm seemed unperturbed by me. While they were angry about what I represented, because my racism was so blatant they knew where I stood. Hence, I was not threatening to them. What astonished me was how lovingly they responded to me. Here I was, unable to feel love for myself, but they still treated me kindly.

Everything came tumbling down for me as Gloria spoke of the pain that came from loving a white man. For the first time I was feeling for a black woman and was able to feel disgust, not for her, but for my prejudice, which is where my abhorrence belonged. I felt ashamed, especially since the racism of my people and me was the source of the suffering she and her people experienced.

When Gloria shared her feelings, she captured my heart. I craved to hold and comfort her as if she was my own. This took my racist view and shattered it. This truly special person had deep feelings for her man and was willing to lose all just to be with him. That was the price she had to pay for the freedom to love. I had always assumed mixed couples were making a political statement and were trying to confront whites with our prejudice. I never dreamed they might simply be in love, and I had no inkling that their love was accompanied by such sacrifice and struggle. Once I recognized this, I could not remain silent any longer.

I told Gloria the feelings I had, how I was attracted to her, my disgust, my prejudices, my shame, my empathy. I held nothing back. She listened and accepted me in a way I never expected. By the end my heart ached for her, and I desperately wanted her to have a life filled with love. I told her this. I also thanked her for accepting me as a person and for making it clear to me that she would not tolerate my racism.

I promised her, "Gloria, never again will I let the awful feelings I have about others or myself go unchallenged. I will always carry vivid images of you, Crystal, and Latania, three beautiful women of African descent who taught me what it means to love. You will always be there in my heart, reminding me when I have ugly feelings about others, to work on cleansing myself. I will carry with me the assurance that even when I could not love myself, you accepted me and showed me I could rise above my base self even when I thought it was not possible. Most of all, I will remember that you gave me your honesty and your love not because of what I am, but because of what you are."

## Sharon: Firm as the Ancient Earth

I was one of the three women in the Elite group. At first I was quiet, but soon others found that the currents gushing beneath my calm surface were forceful. I am Japanese American. My family has lived in the United States for generations and my people have a long history of being marginalized in this land of our birth. Hence, as an Elite, I wanted to create a society where no one felt shunned. I discovered that running a system was demanding and exhausting. I knew there would be extreme differences among the groups and the inequities would be tough to manage, but I had no idea how awesome it would feel to actually be responsible for what happened.

We Elites were given a huge problem to address: what to do with the homeless. We felt we must look after them. Having such a concrete problem led us to think the Outs were our biggest challenge. That was not true. Our real dilemma was how to create a viable system out of the energies everyone brought to the Farm. Focusing on the homeless led us to adopt a reactive posture from which we never escaped, despite our endless discussions about the need to be proactive.

There were some dreadful traps we built for ourselves. For example, consensus decision making was impossible for us Elites because we could not agree on anything. However, I wanted consensus so we would all be forced to share the blame when things went wrong. We wanted to do the right thing, but actually we tried not to do the wrong thing. Our group was driven mostly by fear. When I saw this, many things came into focus for me. Two words stick out about my Farm experience: guilt and fear. How easily the Outs could sway us by using guilt tactics.

Fear and guilt are the two emotions that have paralyzed the Japanese American community since its internment during World War II. What an ordeal this was! One day all the men of my grandfather's generation were arrested, placed on trains with boarded-up windows, and sent away to work camps. They had been made prisoners. A few days later all the Japanese women and children were to be sent away too. What an outrageous act. There were Germans and Italians in many neighborhoods, schools, factories, and offices across the country. Did their bloodlines not put them equally on the side of the enemy? So why was it only the Japanese who were being herded off like cattle?

For generations my people had viewed themselves as Americans who happened to have Japanese ancestors. The war forced them to accentuate their Japaneseness again. Overnight it was evident that adjusting to the dominant culture counted for naught when the crisis hit. Being interned together led them to revert to their Japanese roots, a fact that was deviously used as an indication they were less patriotic than other immigrant Americans.

This piece of our nation's tortured history created a dilemma for my people. The strength of the Japanese American community came from our togetherness and our belief that by living in union with all things we would be at peace. Yet the bombing of Pearl Harbor clashed fiercely with such a view. Japan's aggression was a betrayal of how the Japanese in America had been living for generations. This was too much for America to deal with, but it was also too much for my people, whose liberties were stripped from them and whose property was flagrantly stolen.

During the 1980s my community fought hard for reparations. While I know that interning American citizens of Japanese ancestry was unjust and unconstitutional, my people used guilt as our main tactic in seeking monetary reparations from the U.S. government. This created two dilemmas: Did this tactic settle or rekindle the animosity toward my race? And what impact did it have on Japanese Americans to be fixated on our resentment for so long, seeking a vindication that could only be symbolic?

Fear drove every aspect of this awful episode. It was fear that compelled the U.S. government to lock up Japanese Americans in the 1940s, fear they would undermine the American war effort, even though many Japanese joined the U.S. forces and became gallant soldiers. And for my community this whole period was defined by fear, fear over the loss of life and liberty, fear of being stripped of our legal rights, fear that we would never find a place in this society again, fear that such an injustice would be repeated if a similar circumstance arose again.

Fear also drove my every action at the Farm. I was afraid I would be unable to handle the responsibilities and pressures of my Elite position, afraid I would embarrass myself before my peers, afraid there would be a revolution if we did not run the society right. And then there was the issue of how we dealt with Blair. He kept reminding us that we were being driven by our fear. That was too much. Rather than accept the truths he was reflecting back to us, we projected onto him all the things we wanted to ignore about ourselves, and we drove him away.

It was scary to see how much stuff I imported into the Farm from other parts of my life. Many of my reactions were unrelated to what happened at the time but were leftover feelings I had from previous situations. It was as if I was living in a perpetual state of emotional jet lag. My responses were not an authentic reaction to that moment but were an expression of some unresolved, unrecognized residue of an earlier event unrelated to the present. When I saw how all-pervasive this was I felt guilty.

During the review I recognized how the resentment I carry in me blocks me from seeing the people around me as they are. I also realized that by judging others I indict myself; I displace some aspect of me I disavow, relocate it in them, and then hold them accountable for things I myself am avoiding. My challenge now — and I feel exhilarated by this task — is to recognize my judgmentalism for what it is: my attempt to rid myself of fear and guilt. Henceforth, when I catch myself judging anyone, I will ask what I am afraid of and what my guilt is about. I now know there is nothing to be afraid of except my fear, and nothing to feel guilty about except for the destructive ways I dispose of my guilt.

Despite all we went through, the Farm community was made up of people who were understanding, empathic, and concerned for each other's well-being. It was an ordeal, but as emotionally lost people we learned how to be at home with each other and with ourselves.

## Suffering the Insults

I listened with tear-filled eyes to Gloria, Lee Wan, Johannes, and Sharon as they spoke of their attempts to create a meaningful life in contexts that stifled the spirit. Their pain highlighted how racism brings anguish to our world but is also an inner curse that is hard to purge. It is like a chronic disease that can flare up unexpectedly at any time. We have to be ever mindful of its presence and work to keep its lethal force contained.[18] The fear and guilt that permeated the stories of these four participants felt familiar, for I too had wrestled with these tough emotions. I also had been touched by racism's cruel hand. Early on I realized that my racism was rooted not only in the projections I engaged, but in the collective projections of the people around me. I knew I should rid myself of it for the sake of those who were the target of my enmity. But not until I recognized that I was the person most burdened by my racism did I seriously begin work on this. When I saw that my own well-being was at stake, the desire to free myself became stronger than the guilt paralyzing me.

The aspect of my racism that was hardest for me to deal with was how I felt about the Chinese and the Japanese. The China part was easy to grasp. My family could have died at the hands of the Chinese as their revolution broke. Also, my dad made no bones about his contempt for the communists. He knew their brutality and was opposed to everything they stood for. In his nightmares during my growing-up years in Australia he was always running away from the "Reds," as he called them. Then between 1949 and 1972, the years of China's intense isolation from the rest of the world, the West treated all communist states as the enemy. Although my prejudices toward the Chinese were wrong, I knew their origins.

The Japanese were a different story. I grew up thinking of the Japanese primarily as a force of evil in the world. My early feelings about this nation were shaped by my extended family. When I was eight I gave my uncle a Christmas present, a small object I bought with a few coins out of my piggy bank. He turned it over, read on the back "Made in Japan," and uttered, "Cheap!" There was no "thank you." That day I learned a new curse word: "Jap!"

For twenty years I looked at every object I was about to buy to see if it was made in Japan. If so, I put it back. For my family, the word "cheap," when applied to the Japanese, was not a temporary state of being. Nor was it a mere attribute of an object made in a place where the people were still economically digging themselves out from the rubble caused by the atomic bomb. "Cheap" was a character flaw, permanently etched into the constitution of a whole people. This was ironic, since today "Made in Japan" is almost a synonym for "quality."

Not until adulthood did I find the origins of my prejudice. By then I knew plenty about World War II, the Japanese incursion into the Pacific, the assault on Pearl Harbor, the threat to North Australia, the vicious fights between the Australian troops and the Japanese on the Kokoda trail in New Guinea. I also knew one of my uncles, a fighter pilot, had been shot down and become a Japanese prisoner of war. For eighteen months he was held captive, malnourished, tortured, and forced to witness many deaths resulting from prison atrocities. However, I had not known this when I gave him my "cheap" present less than a decade after his release. While that war belonged to an earlier era, its legacies, the good and the bad, cascaded unabated into my generation. Among other things, it taught me not to trust the Japanese, even though I identified with the side that dropped the atomic bomb, obliterating two Japanese cities and killing many innocent civilians. Half a century later, I wonder who was the least trustworthy?

I tried to overcome the prejudices I had about the Japanese, but my disdain for them was not abating and I had no idea why. I stumbled into the reasons when walking down a path unrelated to Japan, at least so I thought. I was talking with my mother about our relationship. Having learned the art of honest talk with her, I resolved to find out why she emotionally withdrew whenever strong emotion was expressed in our family. I approached this anguish of my early years with the energy of a young Sherlock Holmes. My mother seemed open to the connection I was trying to build with her. This conversation occurred when we were in the car, driving alone.

"Mum, I have always been angry with you for your emotional distance and your withdrawal whenever I got upset about something as a kid. Why did you do this?"

She began to weep oh so gently. I thought, "Here we go again; she's going to guilt me for even telling her I used to be angry."

I was determined not to back away this time. I asked, "Why the tears, Mum?"

Her answers stunned me and showed me, in a few minutes, that I had been misjudging her all my life. The conversation was disjointed, for it stirred many emotions, but I learned enough to get close to the core of the mystery before she asked me to back off and accept her need to keep certain things private. This was what I pieced together.

As a twenty-three-year-old she had traveled on top of a coal train in subzero temperatures to a place in Northern China that was soon to become one of the black holes of the ancient world during the Sino-Japanese war of the 1930s. She and one other British woman were the only Caucasians in the village when Japanese troops arrived. She was terrified and hid, but was soon found. The soldiers brutally abused her. There was no help. In time physical recovery occurred, and she resumed a full life in that village once the invading army had left. However, the emotional trauma lived on.

By the time she next saw a doctor, she had acquired a blood pressure problem, presumed to be caused by this attack. While this does not make sense from a medical perspective, the doctor led her to believe that she would have elevated blood pressure from that day forth and that the best way to control it was by having a life free of emotional volatility. Otherwise, the risks to her health could be catastrophic. She became convinced that if she did not have a life of tranquility she would face an early death. This was why she hated turbulence in the family and consciously walked away from all conflict. It so happened that her own mother had died when she was eleven months old, after which she lived with her grandmother, who died when she was six. From that point on she was cared for by an aunt. She knew a lot about losing mothers, a fate she wanted to save her children from. So if the doctor said to suppress all turbulent emotions, she would obey his instructions.

"You mean that when I thought you wanted to squash my emotions as a child, you were protecting yourself because you were afraid that if you hung in you might die?" I asked flabbergasted.

She began to sob. "Oh, Kenwyn, I feel so upset. That's true, but things were more complicated than I could ever put into words!"

"What else can you tell me?" I asked excitedly, hoping to crack one of the silent mysteries that had ruled our existence.

"I don't think I can say much else," my mother replied, as her sobs grew beyond her control.

"Over the last few years you have been going bald. Is that related to how you were treated by the Japanese?"

"I don't know, but probably. Certainly I think about it every time I put on my wig. They pulled out every hair on my head by the roots! It took so long to grow back. At the time it hurt terribly. Now almost all of my hair has fallen out!"

I was stunned to see my mum, who had been so emotionally regulated, falling apart before my eyes. I also knew this conversation was the beginning of a change in our relationship.

"Kenwyn, I don't think I can tell you all you want to know. Some things a mother should not share with a son. It has been impossible to talk about it with anyone, especially your father."

"You mean Dad doesn't know?"

"He's got a vague sense of it, but you're asking me details I have not told him."

I recognized I was about to go over the edge she had asked me to respect. I pulled the car over, and we had the warmest embrace. "Any time you want to tell me more I would like to hear it, but I will not pry further," I said. That day I got insight about many things, although it was still to be years before I experienced the healing with my mother my floundering spirit craved.

Unexpectedly, I had stumbled upon the emotional base for my prejudice toward the Japanese. I knew these feelings would not magically subside, and, while they were unacceptable, I knew why they existed. That was a start. However, as my mother let me know about her vulnerability, she, I, and our relationship was nourished. It did not bring immediate peace, but the growth begun in both of us that day grew and grew, coming to a rich culmination at her death. What a joy it was to silently weep with Sharon as she told of how lost she and her people were in the United States and to feel that she was a soul sister around whom I instinctively wrapped my arms. A poison of my yesteryears had become a healing balm. I inwardly wept again for my mother and her anguish, and for the blessings that had come to our relationship before she died.

•

On that morning in 1984, when my brother and I were standing in front of our old house in Chengdu for the first time since we were young children, we lost contact with our father for a few minutes. He had found a man he had known back in the 1940s. We assumed the two of them were having an enjoyable chat about the past. But their exchange had got Dad both excited and disturbed. Suddenly he rushed over to us as quickly as his seventy-five-year-old, Parkinson's-filled body would permit and said, hyperventilating, "He recognizes me. We've got to get out of here!" My brother and I were so engrossed in the scenes of our childhood, we failed to notice what had happened to our father. For him, it was no longer 1984. He was back in 1949 and had begun to fall apart. He was convinced he was about to be captured by the communists. We had a potential disaster on our hands and thought we should get him out of the immediate area. We hoped that would jar him out of the deep regression into which he was falling. However, the fuse had been lit in him, and there was nothing we could do to stop the inner implosion about to occur.

Over the next few hours our father entered a period of full-blown paranoia. Every time the driver stopped, even at a traffic light, Dad expected to be dragged from the van by police or troops or secret agents. He saw danger everywhere, even though the only things we noticed were normal people doing the chores of daily life. Within hours he was in a serious crisis. Of course, his age and illness made it hard to tease apart exactly what was going on.

That afternoon we were scheduled to fly from Chengdu to Xian. Dad was eager to get to the airport as fast as possible. We had visited all the sites in this city that were important to us — my brother's first school, the hospital where my siblings had been born, etc. — and were willing to accommodate Dad's wish to be gone from the place that had been so traumatic for him three and a half decades earlier. He was convinced that if we could just make it out of town they would not catch him. He was equally sure that if we stayed any longer in this hostile place we'd never escape.

This had become a horrible day for my father. I was sad. For so long he had yearned to be back in China, to be surrounded by the sounds, sights, and smells that had defined the very concept of familiarity for the first twenty years of his adult life. It was horrible that, once he was there, the old fears that had traumatized him for thirty-five years could not be stilled long enough for him to enjoy the moment. However, everything occurring before my eyes was to make a huge contribution to the inner changes I had craved all my life. Being at the scene of my childhood trauma, my version of ground zero, and seeing with great clarity the emotional rubble created by my dad's terror, convinced me that my lifelong anxieties had been about something real. The old amorphous forces, which I had been unable to grasp because they had been denied, had become as real as my own flesh: we were at the old house; Dad had regressed, psychologically, to 1949; we had to run; the communists were after us! In an instant all that my parents had tried to pretend was not real, in the hope of preventing us children from being traumatized, was staring me in the face. That day Dad's decompensation showed me what I had always known in my bones: my fears were based on reality. That was a great gift to me.

We made it out of Chengdu. However, just as had been the case in 1949, the fears Dad thought he could leave behind went with him. His paranoia did not fade once we were in Xian. The terrors stirred by his yesterdays grew stronger, shaking the foundation of his physiological system and making his Parkinson's disease seem mild in comparison. Within a day we were wondering if we should fly him back to Australia in an air ambulance.

For the first twenty-four hours after leaving Chengdu Dad was up and down like an unregulated elevator. I knew he was physically safe; that was not the issue. I had covered all the necessary diplomatic bases. He was no longer designated an enemy. His name had been taken off all lists. Before our departure for China Dad had never mentioned any concerns about security. I had been the one who was worried about this, and my fears had propelled me to put in place all the necessary political and legal assurances we might need. Also, no one was looking at him askance. No one was threatening him. In fact almost every Chinese person who saw his distress was concerned about his well-being and was asking how they could help.

I decided to see if it was possible to actually prick the bubble of his paranoia. "What are you so afraid of Dad? Why do you think they'll get you? What did you do to make them so angry that they would still want to kill you thirty-five years later?" Bit by bit, he began to let out details that helped me see why the Chinese communists might have deemed him an enemy of the people. Dad obviously felt guilty about something, but if he knew it, he wasn't saying. I pushed as hard as I could to get to the bottom of it, hoping that if Dad could say aloud his truth it would help him move psychologically. However, his disintegration had become so severe my brother and I even wondered if he was on the verge of a coronary. My brother asked me to back off on my truth quest, and we started thinking about medical help. However, my dad would not see just any doctor; his paranoia would not let him fall for that. We were caught in several conundrums, not least of which was the thought that he might have wanted to come to China to die.

Somehow Dad managed to hang on through the next day, when we were scheduled to fly to Beijing. If we could make it to this metropolis we had many more options. It is worth noting that, even in 1984, there were very few places in China open to foreigners. For example, in each city we had visited there was only one hotel available to foreigners, and it usually accommodated only a few guests. Options were limited. China was in the earliest stages of ending its isolation from the world. There were few cars and no services to outsiders. It was a far, far cry from today's China. In the midafternoon, a few hours before our flight to Beijing, Dad took a turn for the worse. We thought he was going to have a heart attack. Our driver, convinced Dad could not proceed, turned to him and, speaking in Mandarin, insisted on taking Dad to his home, a place with dirt floors and a few temporary walls. This modest man was adamant that he would look after my father until he was well enough to continue.

I watched in amazement as this man, whom my dad's paranoid self had insisted was an enemy who would kill him if he knew his name, in a kind and gentle way penetrated the walls of my dad's defenses. A man, hired for a minimal wage to drive a van for a few strangers and seen by my father as an adversary, extended his loving arms to a troubled foreigner. His offer was so genuine even a paranoid got the message. And I marveled at a truth passed on down through the ages: that the love and care of the enemy can be a profoundly healing force.

We made it to Beijing, although during the whole flight I sat poised to lay Dad in the aisle and do CPR. Later I recognized that our visit to Chengdu had enabled my dad's suffering self to escape from the inner closet where it had been kept captive for so long. Problematic though this was, this journey was in part about giving our dad the opportunity to pick up the projections he'd left behind thirty-five years before.

*Thy right hand will hold me fast.*
Psalm 139:10

# Chapter 8

# Liberating Containers

It is normal to seek outlets for the conflicts raging within. When tensions result from the Out and Elite selves banging against each other, it is understandable why fleeing, stealing, and projecting occur. However, when these escape mechanisms don't work, people often implode. This happens when emotions such as rage, abandonment, dismay, and fear get turned back on the self.

In this chapter we meet four people who dealt with the conflicts between their creative and suffering selves by imploding. For Edwin and Joshua it took the form of long-term emotional withdrawal. The explosive dynamics of the Farm somehow released the feelings that had been eating away at them. With Ruth, the implosion became manifest as bodily symptoms that were emotionally and physically debilitating. For Boris, his way of managing his life pathos was to close down his external relationships.

As Boris, Ruth, Edwin, and Joshua accepted the realities of their suffering selves they opened themselves to the creative forces that had been growing in the shadows. This liberated them from containers that had kept them safe but boxed them in. Yet important discoveries had been incubating during this period and were released when they found the accepting self, the version of the self that does not stifle or invalidate the tensions coming from the soul's polarities.

## Boris: From Whence Cometh My Help

The first part of this course was awful for me. I was so alone. I liked people in this class. But no one knew what was in my

119

heart. Others did not understand. No one listened to me. I was awkward all the time. It was not that I did not try. When others emote, I think. I feel so much. It aches in me. But I didn't have the words for the feelings. Their words meant little to me. And my words I gagged on. Ah, words! My prison since I was fourteen.

That was the year my family emigrated from the Soviet Union. We were political refugees, Jews who could no longer tolerate our homeland. What does that word mean, "homeland"! How can a place be home when you cannot live there without fears! We had to leave. We came to a new place, where I never fit in either. Can a place be home when people cannot know your heart because you cannot say what is in it? I do not have the words. They laugh and I do not know what is funny. I gave up asking them to explain. I hide that I do not know what is humorous. Worse, you laugh when they are serious. That's me. I try hard not to, but how can you not laugh when it is funny? What is life without laughter?

In class, timing was a big problem. The others raced ahead but I was minutes behind. I had intellectual jet lag. I could not catch up. When they talked I noticed how different I was. I tried to say what was the same in me. Yet my attempts to say "me too" made it obvious there was no "me too." No one was cruel. They just ignored me. I was excluded and no one cared. They had no reserves for me. My experience, my life, was so different.

Four weeks after my arrival here and one week after entering a Brooklyn high school, I was in a riot. The black and Italian students were in combat. I was forced to choose sides. I did not know the issues. Why was I to hate the kids the Italians called the "n" word? Or why should I throw rocks at "wops"? There I was, crouched behind an overturned school bus hurling rocks at who knows whom. I had no idea why we riot. That made me feel out. Those who could not relate to me gave up on me, even a mugger! A kid came at me with a knife. He wanted my lunch money. He talked fast. I did not understand a word. I muttered, "Good knife, me Boris, how do you do, weather is warm." He left in disgust.

It was the same in Ukraine. In the country of my birth, I was a political refugee, without citizenship, rights, or recourse to justice and protection. We were pawns in the hand of politicians. Jews in the Soviet Union had no rights. For me it was more horrible. I never knew I was a Jew until I was eight. As a child I had been taught to hate the Jews and to harass Jewish children. Then one day I learned I was one of them. Overnight I became the object of my hatred. It was hard to be a Jew there. On the first chance we fled to the United States. Again, we had to live with former enemies.

A decade later history turned me into a man who came from a country that no longer existed. When asked, "Where do you come from?" I couldn't answer. I was born in the Ukraine, but do not call me Ukrainian. I don't consider myself one of them, given the atrocities they did to my people. My native tongue was Russian, but I never lived in Russia. Bitter irony: for much of my life I wished my Soviet passport said I was Russian and not a Jew. Then I wished it said I was a Jew, and not a Russian.

When people speak emotions, I cannot say what is in me. It is in the gut first, or is it the heart? Then you try to explain yourself by slicing away the unexplainable and the inexpressible, forcing its truncated image into the mind. Then you mold and rape and sterilize that emotion until it's articulated. Then you communicate it. Then you look around for a reaction and see empty stares. Then you feel like a fool for having said so little, while feeling so much. Sometimes I want to express my anger or my pain. It is eating away at me. Yet what comes out is a sterilized, eviscerated, shadowy caricature of my feelings. It is so pathetic I am disgusted with the shallowness of my expressed emotions, their ugliness, their nakedness, their incompleteness. I choke them back inside where they can remain unspoiled by language.

When I came to America another filter imposed itself between my naked emotions and their verbal manifestations. I went around dutifully translating from heart to mind, from Russian to English, sounding like a cartoon character. Then, unfortunately, I learned English. Unfortunately because I gave up on improving my Russian and surrendered the one chance I had to clearly say my emotions. When I think "water" in English, it is no more than a combination of letters. It is antiseptic and removed. When I think "voda" (Russian for water), the images of wetness, splashing, thirst, are in my mind. The imagery is far richer and far more tangible than five letters *w-a-t-e-r.*

I never said to my fiancée, "I love you" in Russian. Recently I picked up the phone to do this and hung up three times. "I love you" in Russian has such powerful imagery. It is so primordial! I am afraid to know if I love in Russian with the "shiver down my back, sinking gut" feelings. Maybe I can only love in English.

I feel in Russian. I think in English. My Russian is that of a fourteen-year-old, not enough for adult emotions. I have no words in Russian to capture feelings like longing and nostalgia. I resort to English and lose visceral connection with the emotion. My emotions lose their "emotionness" and become mere words, hollow phrases. I lose ownership of what I say and find no relief in saying it. Sometimes when I express an idea, language pre-empts emotion and I don't know which is which. If I cannot find a word that sounds right, in a rush to complete a begun sentence I use the next best substitute, altering what I wanted to say. When I finish a thought, I am in a different place than where I want to be. I then alter my emotions to fit my words. This creates a dissonance between what I think I feel and what I feel. The more complex the emotion, the greater the dissonance. That creates new emotions, which again become misinterpreted by the time they are articulated. This vicious cycle rules my emotional life.

It was right that I was homeless at the Farm. That's what I have always been. I took my place in this group and listened to my fellow Outs who all had their versions of being without a home. It helped that we never needed to say how we felt. We all felt the same. We got upset by the same things, laughed at the same things, got comforted by the same things. Every attempt to say what anyone thought or felt brought a chorus of agreement.

In day-to-day life we Outs had little in common. But in the shelter we found we had in common our lack of commonness. In life we all felt alienated. We did not know how to connect. We were not at home in the world. That made us at home with each other.

It was never easy for me. Even with the Outs. Someone would talk about his futile quest to find a home. This touched a scar so deep in me I could not hold back. I had to speak. However, while the emotional upheaval rocked my body back and forth, I could utter only a couple of words, all the time choking back the spasms in my throat. Someone suggested I say it in Russian. If only I could! But I forgot, or never knew how. Hence, my grief.

During the review I tried to speak but froze. I felt angry and wanted to strike out. I threw my anger at a staff person. I expected him to be angry back. His response surprised me.

"Boris, I have been moved by you. I was holding in my tears when you told us that as a child you were taught to hate Jews and then discovered you were a Jew. How do you come to love the parts of you that you have been taught to hate? Then your family fled the Soviet persecution of Jews and you ended up in a country that had been taught to hate everything about the place from whence you had come. How does a boy find a home in this setting? In a way I've always known you, because you came from a country I was taught to fear and hate. That's why our weapons were permanently aimed at your people. I knew you because we only hate those who remind of us of ourselves. You were part of what Ronald Reagan called the Evil Empire. How wonderful to have you here making it obvious that people living in a different political system are not evil just because they are in a different political system. You help us all to get new perspectives on ourselves, and I thank you."

## Ruth: I Will Not Sleep Until I Find Sanctuary

From the beginning, I was a controversial person in this class, acting in ways that made others think of me as needy. I put out "I want you to pay attention to me" messages, but when they responded, I accused them of being intrusive. For example, one day I dressed provocatively. It was only a matter of time before some guy commented that he did not take me seriously because of my clothes. I was on him right away. I accused him of being sexist and demanding that I behave in a way that made him comfortable. Soon everyone was into a debate about gender dynamics. I sat back and smiled. I liked being the center of attention and doing it in a way that threw others off center.

At the Farm, I was a Middle. Given the benevolence of the Elites this was no hardship. My dilemma was being caught up in the male-female dynamic within our Middle group. Together with two other women, both African Americans, I had to contend with the out-of-control energy of the Middle men. They advocated that all have an equal voice in how the society ran but were autocrats in our group. To get their voices heard they were willing to silence us Middle women.

We coped by creating a strong sense of sisterhood. It was new for me to be the sole white bonding with two black women, especially ones who demanded I pull my emotional weight. They would not tolerate game playing from me. They were interested only in the real me. My choice was clear: get real or get left behind. My typical way of influencing others was summarily dismissed. This was the shock therapy I needed.

I began discovering sides of me I did not know. For years, I'd worked to look attractive on the outside to compensate for how ugly I felt on the inside. However, I'd never had the courage to look at my inner self before. At the Farm I peeked inside. Instead of finding a repulsive monster I found a person who was terrified of being alone in this world and who shut people out to protect against being hurt. But in the process, I had also closed myself off to me.

I assumed that having no pain would make me happy. However, my efforts to avoid pain were killing my spirit. My wish for a pain-free existence was blocking my sadness, my anxiety, my uncertainty, my emotions. With the help of the Middle women, I broke through the defenses that had anesthetized me. Instead of protecting myself I let myself be caught up in the turbulence around me. This made me feel raw, but the payoff was a steady stream of clear emotions. I saw that I was a wounded person in need of help. For some time I had suffered from two ailments, what doctors call an "eating disorder" and a "sleep disorder." These diseases had been with me so long I had stopped thinking of them as either problematic or as something that could be cured.

Farm life showed me that my eating disorder was connected to a distorted image I had of my body. I felt heavy and this made me think I was fat. Actually, my size was fine. However, I carried a huge weight. It was not the result of excess calories I took in, but of impacted emotions I failed to discard. To reduce my heaviness I obsessively calculated the grams of fat in every bit of food and how much I had to exercise to burn off what I ate. I went to the gym and pushed myself to the limits. I was haunted by my fear that, as my body deteriorated, my worth would fade. I was so afraid of empty tomorrows I dedicated my todays to protecting myself from that eventuality, thereby filling each day with the very vacuousness I wanted to avoid.

I had created an impossible bind. I was always wanting men's assurance of my beauty, yet when a man did compliment me I acted as if he only wanted me for my body, and if I let him get close, he would not like me and I'd feel ugly again. Or I'd think he was just looking at me on the surface level, and who would want a man who was so superficial? I worked to ensure that men never gave me negative images of my body, yet I dismissed their compliments.

Forming tight bonds with women helped me forget about men for a while. Latania and Crystal didn't care what I looked like. Their only interest was in the quality of my spirit, and from their point of view that was fine. When we came to the review session external appearances faded for all of us. The only things we were looking at were our interiors.

Life at the Farm showed me what a control freak I was. My efforts to make everything play out as I wanted were exhausting me. For the previous twelve months, although I was overtired, I rarely slept. When I did doze off I tossed and turned or sleepwalked.

For weeks after being at the Farm my emotions vacillated wildly, but it was wonderful to feel my life pulsating through me. Having the good and the bad side by side restored my vitality. I laughed and cried and sometimes felt like a mess, but I was alive. Before I was flat and calculating and dull. I had covered over my wounds, but they were festering out of my field of vision. I had needed others' help but had locked myself in my own cocoon. I broke out of my excessive exercise regime and altered how I relate to food, adopting the attitude of "so what if I carry a few more pounds on my body." I began exercising in moderation and eating in moderation and living a more balanced life. This brought the gift of sleep. Actually, the day I got back from the Farm I knew my struggle with sleep was over. As I got into bed that night, I felt at peace for the first time since childhood. I knew I would sleep well that night, and it has continued.

I have thought a lot about what contributed to the end of my eating and sleep disorders. Several things stand out. I no longer try to control how people react to me. I once had many routines I used to produce the responses I wanted. I thought this would make me more likeable. What a shock to discover no one likes me when I do this, but that people do accept me when I'm being myself. How freeing to discover my likeability resides in me and not in others.

I also discovered that I am more comfortable with women than men. That was new. I always had a difficult time with women friends. Even casual female acquaintances seemed competitive, jealous, and petty. Of course, it was me who was this way, not them. As I changed, my experience of others changed! Although I feel closer to people and value more what we have in common, I also feel more connected to my individuality than ever.

During a conversation I had with a staff member from the Lab, she said something that became a powerful symbol for me. I was saying how delighted I was about being able to sleep though the night. She commented, "Perhaps you had to wake up in order to go to sleep." That captured it all for me. Waking up as a human being let me sleep like a lamb.

## Edwin: Grief Dims My Eyes

Being a Middle was perfect because I felt "in between" in all areas of life. As a twenty-six-year-old Chinese American who had it made (Exeter, Harvard, Wall Street, sudden wealth, Wharton) when I listened to my peers in the homeless shelter I was sad. I realized that the more successful I had become, the more lost I felt. I had to find out what made me so out of sorts with myself.

Unexpectedly, I found it was because I had lost all contact with my Asian roots.

As others spoke about feeling forsaken by their families, I flashed to when I was sixteen. It was the start of the school year, and my parents had just dropped me off at Exeter. They had sold the family home, were leaving the United States where they had been all their lives, and were moving to Hong Kong. I felt abandoned, ran into my room, and cried for hours. When my tears dried I started ten years of withdrawal from which I refused to emerge. I was angry with my parents and retaliated by closing myself off from them and deciding to never trust anyone again.

After reliving these emotions I called my parents in Hong Kong and told them how upset I had been when they left me in boarding school in the United States and returned to Asia. They did not understand why I was distressed, but that didn't matter. I was being honest with them at last, and this helped me to start being emotionally honest with myself. My failure to be truthful about my feelings was crippling me. In the past when a feeling surfaced, my reaction was, "Is this emotional response reasonable? If not, change it." That created all kinds of trouble. How crazy to think that emotions could be regulated by the mind!

Speaking with my parents was important, but it was not them I wanted to be reunited with. It was reconnecting with the lost parts of myself that was important. Soon I saw that it was my lack of connection to my Chinese heritage that distressed me most. My parents had left ten years before to reestablish their ties with Asia. I needed that reintegration too, but I had been so out of touch with my roots I didn't even know I was out of touch. Half of me had been left behind as I'd grown.

This paralleled another problem. I was so engrossed in the rational that my intuitive side never developed. Mathematics, science, and logic had ruled my life, while my emotional and spiritual self had no visible role in my development. My life existed solely in the material and rational domain. The expressive was a foreigner. I even thought that the more money you have the more loved you are, that everything could be reduced to economic terms.

After a few weeks musing on these issues, a friend commented that I was sounding Chinese for the first time. I understood what he meant and decided to actively explore Chinese philosophy. I began with the concept of balance, something I did not have. Soon I was seeing the yin and the yang everywhere. I read the copy of Lao Tsu's *Tao Te Ching* that my college roommate had given me at graduation. I had never even opened it! The words leapt out at me. I felt them and wept. Page after page spoke to me like nothing had before. I knew then that I had to embrace my Chinese heritage to feel whole. It was one thing to succeed in America, but I had lost contact with my ancestry and it was time to reverse this.

I decided to pursue a business career that involved working in China, Korea, and Japan. I was excited because this would force me to explore my origins. I also confronted my fear about whether I could trust white males. I called a friend and approached this dilemma directly. I said, "You are always nice to me. I have no idea whether you genuinely feel kindly toward me or whether, as a member of the white male elite, you are just compensating for your racism and patronizing me. You are too pleasant with me. I don't trust it. Perhaps if we got upset with each other and our friendship did not fall apart, I'd believe it!"

As I made this statement I noticed the many projections I was flinging at my friend. All my life I had expected to be treated poorly. If someone was kind, I viewed it as fake because I didn't think I was worthy of acceptance. During this call I saw my wish to be validated by the white male elite establishment. I also realized I didn't allow white males to be what they were, men with self-doubt and a need of acceptance just like me.

I was also concerned about my overall level of fatigue. For months I had been exhausted, finding it increasingly difficult to rise in the morning. I was depressed. It was as if my spirit was afraid to wake. It became easier to stay asleep. Only when I accepted how afraid I was did my vitality return. Instead of sleeping long and waking tired, I began to bounce out of bed each morning after just a few hours of sleep. I also confronted my main addiction — money — and began doubting if I wanted to continue with my career in finance. I lost my desire for riches and decided I did not want to work with people who were dedicated to the accumulation of money but had no idea how to live a life with any wealth in it.

Another discovery came from my fiancée's wish to be married in a church. I was alienated from religion and did not want my integrity compromised on our wedding day. She argued that I rejected things without examining them. Her claim was valid, and I agreed to go to a regular church service. I liked it. I had not been to church since I was twelve. During the service I was thinking about hypocrisy, both in the church and in me, until the sermon. It was Lent and the preacher suggested this was a time many feel guilty, but he proposed that we think of this as a time to celebrate the capacity given to us all to re-form our lives, to embrace new beginnings. He suggested that instead of feeling bad about the walls we built, to appreciate they were constructed for good reason but have outlived their usefulness. By lowering those walls and letting the light shine on dark places, the possibility for new beginning is born. That sermon was meant for me. Instead of feeling fragmented, I left feeling whole.

What a great few weeks this proved to be: I met myself as an adult and found how Christianity and Taoism could jointly nourish me.

## Joshua: A Heart That Thirsts

The Farm gave me the most intense intellectual, emotional, and spiritual roller coaster ride of my life. This experience defies description, especially the strength of the bonds created among the Middles. Our group had great diversity, yet the relationships we built gave me the stimulus I needed. When a friend asked me what being at the Farm had meant to me, this was what I said: "I walked into a room of twenty-four virtual strangers. My first thought was that not one of these people was likely to have any place in my future. However, the reality is that if any one of this community, even fifty years from now, were to call me and say 'Joshua, I need your help, will you come and be with me?' I would go. If it meant spending a thousand dollars on an airfare, I would go. I might question my sanity blowing the thousand dollars, but the real insanity would be not going. I would go. I believe every one of us would respond the same way." The last day of the review was my birthday. Not only did I turn twenty-eight that day, but I started life anew. Since then I have been racing through a new and exciting emotional childhood.

One event stands as a symbol of the changes born in me at the Farm. The other morning Edwin called at 7:30 just to talk. He asked me for some personal advice. As we spoke he began to sob. I listened with an open heart, and he held nothing back. Somewhere in that conversation I realized I mattered to him, my opinions, my emotions, me. I mattered to him! This was what I'd been searching for all my life — to matter! I had not seen before how desperately I want to matter to others. Edwin let me know that I mattered to him. I don't recall what we discussed, but the insight I got about my needing to matter started me on a new path.

I always sensed something was lacking in me, but I never knew what it was. I found it was the longing for connection. As Edwin and I talked that morning I thought of a long-forgotten event: When I was ten, my mom was hospitalized for a few weeks; by the time she came home, I had withdrawn. I had taken a part of me and buried it, so I wouldn't let myself get hurt again. Well, what got buried long ago has been brought out. When it emerged I felt hurt and raw, but it was the kind of ache that is enlivening. The pain of trying to avoid being wounded was far more soul-destroying.

A few days after we left the Farm I hit the ground with a thud. My emotional high was followed by a period of depression, as I wondered if we had been through something real or if it was just a figment of our imaginations. Having discovered what being connected to other people felt like, my standards for relating had permanently changed. I wondered if I could establish this kind of connectedness with others in everyday life, or if I would end up living in complete frustration, searching for something that did not exist other than at the Farm and in my mind.

Once I had come down from my emotional high, I was anxious about things that had never bothered me. I knew the source of my distress, but insight did not diminish the hurt. However, I had discovered that pain was an essential part of the renewal of life. That gave me fresh ways to relate to my quandaries. I resolved never again to take an emotional aspirin, and I would treat anything that afflicted me as my companion.

One thing that happened to me was a sexual awakening, unlike anything I had experienced. My sensuality was out of control. For weeks I was obsessed with a woman I felt sure was to be my life companion, but she seemed unaffected by my amorous advances. She let me know she liked me, but she also kept her distance. My loins had never felt this form of intensity before. I was certain it was more than the stirrings of young romance. Its very unfamiliarity threw me. I wrestled for days with how to get a handle on feelings that I could not pigeonhole. Having never felt this way I assumed it was because of some special quality in this woman. It took me weeks to realize this was the result of the changes occurring in me. I was developing new capacities to feel, and something as simple as normal lust for a beautiful woman felt like the love of the gods. She was not a goddess and I was not Zeus, but for a few days it felt that way. I soon left these lofty heights and accepted that this was an element in my rebirthing.

The juxtaposition of these extremes taught me that the range and depth of human emotion was more vast than I had realized: the higher I went, the deeper I could fall, and the deeper I was willing to descend, the greater the heights to which I could soar.

This was a time when everything was changing, but many things were also remaining the same. This was exciting and scary, for I had been afraid these changes might be temporary and that I would soon revert to my old ways. However, I was interacting differently with my friends and my family and was noticing feelings I would normally have blocked from awareness. People told me they liked my new way of relating, and I sure did. For the first time in my twenty-eight years, my emotions had as much validity as my thoughts.

## *Weary with Groaning*

The containers Boris, Ruth, Edwin, and Joshua used to hold in their personal conflicts had actually augmented the explosive power of those conflicts, until the container could no longer keep them in check. That threatened their inner stability and required that these tensions be released. However, the containers had successfully served as protective caretakers until the time of liberation arrived. These individuals had tried to master emotions that were fundamentally uncontrollable. They did this for understandable reasons, but it was only a matter of time before things were going to crash in on themselves, for this kind of inner architecture could keep things in for only so long. By the time we met them, they were keen to escape the binds that had resulted from their attempts to free themselves of their unwanted emotions.

The emotional development of these four Farm participants appeared to have frozen in adolescence. In other regards they had flourished. They had successfully negotiated their way into the adult world and were poised to take on major responsibilities. But they were not emotionally equipped for these burdens. Their minds were ready, but their hearts were not. On the other hand a great deal of inner growth had been going on in their developing spirits, but it had taken place out of sight. Sometimes things incubate inside for years, and when they burst forth in full bloom it looks miraculous. However, it is a normal miracle. For it was developing along, following its own idiosyncratic trajectory, and ultimately was brought to life by a force that cracked open the shell containing it. The Farm was this force for many.

While witnessing the relationship between their suffering and creative selves and their struggle to find their accepting selves, I was thinking about my past relationship with my father. By the time I entered adulthood one word summed up how I felt about him: *resentment!* He had been so absent from my life, his very presence was a painful reminder of the fathering I lacked. I needed a strong man to guide me though the minefields between boyhood and manhood, to initiate me into a mature version of maleness. He simply was not that man.

My father's work defined his life. His income was modest and he toiled hard to provide for his family. From an early age though, I knew that work was his escape, the place to which he fled, and I resented that he was always on the run. I knew his flight had something to do with the communists — not the real ones trying to get elected to a seat on the local city council, but the ones from China that he perpetually carried as ghosts in his mind and that would not let him alone. He'd sit at breakfast, overcome by a sense of gloom, and several times a week mother would pierce the silence with a statement that spoke volumes: "So you spent another night with the Reds," a reference to his nightmares about fleeing China during the revolution. My dad would nod, without even lifting his head. We all felt depressed about his depression.

Eventually I worked out how to escape breakfast time. A bowl of cereal eaten on the run while I gathered my schoolbooks saved me from having to witness this wretched scene. Although we had eluded the physical harm threatened by the terrorists of that era, my family was held hostage by their continual presence in my father's sleep-interrupted nights. I had the bedroom next to my parents and was aware of a parental secret. In his sleep my father would let loose with bloodcurdling screams, which were followed by a plaintive, "Gordon, wake up, it's only a dream!" from my mother. Like Ruth, my dad had to awaken to get the rest he needed.

In my late teens, I developed an eye tic. It was not visible to others but it irritated me to the point of distraction. I did the usual things, like standing in front of a mirror to see if I could catch it and discover the point I had to touch to stop it from firing. It became a challenge to me. Could I develop quick enough reflexes to get it before it had fired ten times, then five times, then a second time? Like the cockroach, it got stronger the more I attempted to master it.

When I knew the battle was lost I tried a new approach. Is my eye tic my body's way of sending me a message about something? If so, what is it? For months, when my eye started to tic, I did not try to suppress it but asked what was going on for me at that time. It began as a game that grew more serious by the day as I sensed I was on to something elusive. Gradually I noticed a pattern. My eye ticked whenever I felt resentment. I had never thought of myself as a resentful person. However, as my eye tic fired away, I recognized there were many things I resented, especially the emotional absence of my dad. I also saw that the antipathy I directed at him was my way of hiding a more basic emotion, anger. Actually it was a seething rage.

My wrath left me with no charity toward my dad. I wanted to run away but could not work out how to do that without taking along all that haunted me. It was the absence of my father, his lack of approval, and his invalidation that hurt me. Fleeing was not going to win his approval or gain the fathering I craved. I made a bold move upon graduating high school. I declared myself financially independent and resolved never again to take a cent from my dad. Until I left the family home for good, I paid my parents the market rate for room and board. I also got through all my university studies without any financial help from my family. This was one of the ways I resolved to dig out from under the rubble of my unexpressed rage at my father.

Of course, my methods to avoid my anger did not work. I was a powder keg in the making, and my furiously firing eye tic was my time clock. The day came when I could hold it all in no longer. I made my move. Like the mindless ways people went into battle during the Civil War, I attacked my father with a full-bodied, frontal attack. It was silly. I had given him an ultimatum: do this or else, which signaled the impending battle and the flank from which I'd be attacking. However, my dad was no neophyte. He saw what I was up to and took me out at the knees before I got started. How I had underestimated him! I thought he'd be a pushover, but he easily disarmed me. I retreated and resolved to launch another attack some time when he wasn't watching.

Dad came in with the big guns. He went even more silent on me, refusing to speak with me. The only thing we said to each other for five years were perfunctory three-second Christmas and birthday greetings. Five years! That was as long as World War II, and this was but a minor skirmish between an enraged son and a stubborn father. At one point, I confided to my mother that my anger at my dad had not subsided. Her response got my attention. "Your father has got the message about how angry you are and is trying to find a way to reach out to you." I didn't buy it! Admittedly, I was living a thousand miles away, but a telephone call from him could get the ball rolling. Of course, I would use any gesture he made as a launching pad for my next salvo at him, but I did want him to respond to me and not let silence rule.

However, I began to notice that as I got clear about my anger, my resentment went down, and my eye tic fired less. Then I discovered my body was telling me that whenever I resented anything, my eye tic fired to remind me of emotions I was avoiding. Today I don't think of my eye tic as an unwelcome visitor. It serves as an indicator of troubling resentment on the horizon and now only appears once or twice a year, faithfully pointing out the hidden poison I am about to spray upon myself and whomever I am targeting. More critically, I have found other ways to detect potential resentments long before they grow big enough to trigger my biological buzzer.

My eye tic was not the only symptom my body was giving off. As far back as I could remember, every four to six weeks I got mouthfuls of canker sores. If I bit my lip while munching an apple my whole mouth would become inflamed with twelve to twenty canker spots. In this regard I was just like my father. This was his affliction too, and family folklore had it that I had inherited the same constitutional flaw as my dad. I even resented him for this.

I ultimately got free of my eye tic and shed my mouthfuls of canker sores as my relationship with my father altered. It took two decades.

It started unexpectedly. I had given up on my dad entirely. He was in Australia and I was in the United States completing my education. The phone rang and it was my dad. I was flabbergasted. This was the first serious call he had made to me in five years. He was brief but what he said communicated volumes. "Son" (I do not recall his ever calling me "son" before), "I want to come to your graduation." I'd known my dad as a miser, unwilling to spend a dollar on anything with no instrumental value. Yet here he was about to spend thousands of dollars and take a month away from work to be alone with me and celebrate my academic achievements. I did not know what to say, but his overture got my attention. He knew how angry I still was with him, but he was coming anyway. I just replied, "I'll pick you up at Kennedy Airport."

That visit was wonderful. I was touched by his pride in me. I was even more moved that, as I unloaded on him all the anger I had stored over the years, he listened, never once becoming defensive. I wanted to know everything about our life in China, about the escape, about his political entanglements, about why he had been a hunted man for so long, about his fear of the communists, about why he had buried himself in his work, about what life was like for him. I asked almost everything that was on my mind. Only two things did I leave untouched, for reasons I did not grasp at the time: What was really going on the day we met when I was two and he spanked me on the streets of Bombay? And was he a CIA agent?

I was thrilled that upon grilling him about his life and all that had silenced us as a family, he was enormously responsive. He let me know how sad he was over not being there as a father for me during my first thirty years, but he was also clear that he would seize every opportunity to relate to me henceforth. I was beyond needing the fathering I once craved, but during that month we spent together my dad and I became good friends. He had been so lost to me he may as well have been dead. Yet here he was breathing life into a relationship waiting to be born.

Four years later I was living in Washington, D.C. Dad called with an air of desperation. He had just learned that he had Parkinson's disease. He asked me to return to Australia as soon as possible to visit him. "I know that all of life will be different for me, and I want someone to talk about it with. I can't discuss it with your mother and, anyway, it's your advice I want." Like Joshua, I was touched that I mattered to him in this way. Not that there was anything I could do for him. He just wanted to talk with me about it. That made me feel special. He added that I was the only one he was confiding in and said, "Don't tell your mother. I don't want to worry her."

"Dad, has it ever occurred to you that she is already worried about you? Why don't you two talk about this?"

"I will when I have to, but not now."

"Okay, but she usually works these things out pretty quickly."

Sometime later my mother commented, "Your father is not doing too bad given his Parkinson's."

"Oh, Dad has talked with you about this at last?"

"No!" she replied. "He's never mentioned a word about it."

"How do you know he has Parkinson's then?" I asked.

"I'm no fool. I see the medication he takes. I know people take these pills for Parkinson's."

I was amazed that they were able to continue living under the canopy of silence that had characterized our family life, although they each had been trying to break the reign of silence in their one-on-one exchanges with me.

Over the next few years I had a lot of contact with my dad. The walls between us were tumbling down. Then I had a setback that rocketed me forward so fast I felt the need to walk gently. During a difficult period of my life, I woke each day feeling frightened. My dreams contained images of people being tortured, of mass graves, of the atrocities associated with a revolution. If a car backfired going past my home I automatically hit the floor. I was overtaken by knee-jerk fear. I knew I was going through delayed post-traumatic stress associated with almost being killed as a child. Strong emotions were welling up in me as I recalled things long repressed.

During this time, I began to systematically examine the impact it had on me to have met my father for the first time when I was two. For so long the only event told about that day was that I received my first paternal spanking. I was in my midthirties and had never unpacked what this time had been like for the others in my family. Also, as I encountered this strange man on the streets of Bombay, I must have been terribly confused. The unfamiliar smells of Asia, the sounds of different languages, the anxiety of the unknown all must have been part of that day. For a long time what actually transpired was not accessible to me. All I knew was the tale as told by my dad during my childhood. In the story's telling, essential elements such as what led him to spank me or what my mother felt about how he was treating her son were never mentioned. The focus was on the punch line, on my capitulation: "Tomorrow I'll let you carry me, Daddy." This was the point when dinner guests would croon about how cute I must have been and I would cringe with embarrassment.

In retrospect, what was left out of the story was as critical as what was said. The emotions of all others on that day were never included. What was everyone else feeling? Father had been a key person in my brother's life for two years, and then he had vanished. They were about to be reunited and must have been excited and nervous. My mother had been alone for two years while raising us boys. How were she and Dad feeling about meeting after such a long separation? It must have been such a briny mixture of relief, joy, guilt, anger, and hope.

I suppose as a child I felt I had no right to give expression to my curiosity about the untold elements of this story. All I knew was that I felt devastated each time it was recounted, even though others acted as if I must be enjoying it. For thirty years I accepted that this account, as narrated, was true. It was a part of my past I had no option but to accept. I did not think to protest when it was about to be retold, even though I knew I was going to be hurt again. Nor did it occur to me to talk about this event with my parents. There was a taboo over this occasion and only certain details were admissible.

I had always been unwilling to rely on anyone. When I was sick I wanted to be left alone. My instinct was to tough it out alone. At some point I began to link my problems with dependency to the story of my meeting my father. As I revisited that tale I wondered about how all the traumas of our life in China were expressed. Recognizing how few outlets existed, I asked whether this ritualistic retelling of my meeting my father had enfolded into it other emotions. Perhaps I, along with this story, had been used as a symbolic way to store several events and emotions too scary to acknowledge or examine. This prospect led me to tell a caring therapist the story of my first father-son encounter over and over again, each time giving expression to a little more of the other family emotions that might have been contained within it.

And then one day I recalled a long-lost memory fragment, which was the missing link. There was one more line that I had forgotten, and I suspect it had been deliberately left out in my dad's telling. After I said to him that first evening, "Tomorrow, I'll let you carry me, Daddy," my father replied forcefully, "Tomorrow you will walk!"

As I recalled this brutal statement, which had apparently shaped my lifetime relationship with my dad and my very being, my floodgates burst. I wept and wept. Not until I was exhausted did my supply of tears temporarily stop. In the middle of my grief, I even wondered if it was possible to cry oneself to death. In hindsight, those tears proved to be the cleansing my inner being needed. When the tears subsided, a new understanding about myself had dawned. My childhood had taught me that relying on others would bring rejection. The pain of this discovery was like a surgeon's knife opening the breastplate. Yet I was grateful for its uncovering. The wound felt deep, but it was clean. No longer were there any illusions. I hurt so much I felt real like never before. Dull aches had given way to acute stinging. From someplace within me came the conviction that it was now possible to be healed. I had never believed that before.

•

Upon his retirement three years later, my father visited me for a month when I was living in Washington, D.C. The trek from Australia had taken its toll, and soon after arriving he got ill and was bedridden for two weeks. During his visit I tended to him like a father normally cares for a child. He let me be his nurse. After two weeks he recovered, and I felt close to him in a new way.

During that visit I decided to push our relationship to the next level and to tell him what it had been like for me being his son. I am not sure what possessed me, but this impulse emerged with conviction, and I had resolved not to suppress such inner messages, especially where my father was concerned. Seeing him so ill had made me wonder how I'd feel if he died and there remained important unsaid things between us.

This turned into a day held precious in my memory. He had been a hard man for me to have as a father, and I knew I had not been all that easy a son, although he'd never said that to me. There were plenty of jagged edges to what I said, and it would have been fine had he reciprocated by telling me how difficult it was to be my father. Instead, he chose to tell me what it had been like being a son to his dad. That day we shared our sonship.

I never knew my grandfather; he died before my birth. I often wondered what he was like. During that conversation I met my grandfather, through the eyes of my dad. That stubborn streak in my father that I found so bothersome (because I possessed it in equal measure) was also a major characteristic of my grandfather. Stubbornness seemed to have been passed on as if genetically prescribed. However, as my dad talked about this obstinacy we all shared, he cast a new light on it. Sure it had brought plenty of anguish into our relationship; however, he showed me that this was much more than mere bullheadedness. It was what gave the will the steely quality that enables one to remain focused on distant destinations while tending to the demands of the present.

My dad's reframing of this troublesome attribute we shared helped me accept a part of me I wanted to exile. I would have never expected to get something of such value from my father right in the midst of what could have been a painful and messy conversation. It took me some months to notice this, but in the wake of that visit from my father and the sharing of our sonship my canker sores disappeared. No doctor could ever tell me why this happened, but I had a clear hypothesis that grew stronger with each passing month of canker-free life. When my mouth was full of canker sores I could hardly speak. Could it be that the emotional toxins I kept in my mouth were poisoning me? I have no proof, but it is now two decades since I have had a mouthful of canker sores. More than just my heart got healed as my relating to my dad was infused with honesty. Years later I told my father about the vanishing of my canker sores and pinned their departure to the date of his visit in 1981. His response was wonderful. "Kenwyn, after that trip my canker sores disappeared too. And I'd had mine for seventy years." Our changing relationship was healing us both.

Looking back, I marvel that the imploding I had done over the years incubated some of the richest things that happened to me. It prepared the way for the birth of my accepting self, whose task it was to integrate all that came from both my creative and suffering selves.

> *Now will I lie down in peace and sleep;*
> *for thou alone, O Lord, makest me live unafraid.*
> Psalm 4:8

# Chapter 9

# *Releasing Abundance*

A natural response to conflict is to hide, for who wants to be the lightning rod for others' aggression? When an armed enemy arrives, hiding is the most natural self-preservation instinct. With threats coming from the fractured self the inclination is also to hide. There are several forms of psychological hiding, such as denial, deception, disassociation, and delusion. These are familiar and normal coping mechanisms that help each person get through the day. However, when inner passions are at war with one another, the wish for resolution can be so strong it is easy to over-rely on hiding, making it likely that a false sense of reality will be created for both self and other.

In this chapter the spotlight falls on Raul, Dale, and Crystal. Dale was an Out. Raul and Crystal were Middles. All three were trying to construct a life in contexts that could tear the most robust apart. In their worlds, it was so hard to remain integrated they often went into emotional hiding just to get by. However, this form of coping took a large toll on them and increased the very anguish they wanted to lessen. Upon recognizing this conundrum, they worked on keeping inner conflicts in balance and discovered that, by ceasing to hide from the truths governing their lives, a new form of inner acceptance emerged, one that helped them feel more whole and more real.

Raul was a black man who was born in Africa but raised in America by a white family. He was a dynamo, packing more energy into a few minutes than most people put into a day. Yet hiding within the whirlwind that surrounded him were several truths he had yet to uncover. Dale was a gay man, living in the midst of the HIV community, who wanted desperately to hide from the angst of AIDS. Crystal was an African American woman who had spent all her years trying to hide from the effects of racism and sexism.

## Raul: Pastures in the Wild

As a Middle it seemed self-evident to me that democracy was the only viable system of governance, so I advocated "one person, one vote." But for the Outs, maintaining solidarity was more important; the things we wanted to be voted on were irrelevant to them. For the Elites, retaining their power was more critical than what they did with that power.

I never meant to hurt anyone. I just wanted everyone to have a say in how we governed ourselves. I was amazed that others saw me as a dangerous man. Some Elites refused to support democracy because they thought it might let me become too influential! They even concluded they would gain more power by opposing me, even though my agenda was the same as theirs: to create a place where everyone belonged.

Some of the animosity I attracted came from past tussles. All semester I had expressed strong opinions and regularly blocked others who tried to pull us in directions I was unwilling to support. I strove to be the leader because I did not want to follow anyone else. But I never did articulate what I would do with the power once I got it.

Looking back, my behavior at the Farm was scary. My political effectiveness was minimal; the harder I pushed, the less willing others were to accept my ideas. Even with the Middles I had to use every technique I knew to get my group lined up behind my plan. Some of the Middles believed that my actions would cause us to lose the only things that made us not Out, a bed by night and meals by day. They would not fight for a cause that cost them their creature comforts. Once I saw that not all Middles were with me, whenever I knew four others would back me up I forced the Middles to vote, and I would win by a five to three margin. I then treated this thin majority as a mandate and rammed my agenda through, making a mockery of my espoused values. I became a person willing to do whatever it took to achieve my ends. I was behaving just like the Elites I wanted to depose.

To get the Outs' support I had to address their concerns and make compromises. However, when the Elites demanded the same from me I got rigid. I thought that to ever be conciliatory with the Elites was tantamount to selling out! My contempt for the Elites limited my ability to influence them. They wanted democracy as much as me, but my actions irritated them so much they became reactionaries. For them, if democracy meant I had any power, better that they become autocrats themselves. Some Outs and a couple of Middles agreed with the Elites on this. I did not see that my contempt for the Farm Elites was a reflection of my contempt for the Elite part of me.

My history had a big role in how I functioned. I was born in Ethiopia during a famine, orphaned at an early age, plucked from nature's carnage by an international relief effort, and adopted by a white American couple. They raised me as one of their own, giving me the best of what the United States has to offer. I am American to my bootstraps, but my soul is tied to the land that gave me birth. I do not accept the world's indifference to the plight of Africa. Be it a war in Somalia, political upheaval in Uganda, AIDS in Nigeria, or famine in the Sudan, I want to help. I am upset by inequality and believe that humanity's problems are perpetuated by the political structures. I want to join the proletariat and fuel the revolution, but I am also eager to use my Elite position and become a politician. I had never seen a way, however, to connect the part of me wanting to tear down that which is destructive and the part of me eagerly trying to create what might be.

The Middle women taught me what I was missing. Despite the huge gender fights in our group, I managed to bond with the women. I was the instigator of what got them riled up and deserved to be the focus of their anger, but they seemed willing to forgive my foibles. I was teflon-coated when it came to the women's wrath, which the other men bore on my behalf. I was grateful but felt sheepish about this when I was with the men. During the review I got some tough feedback and was challenged to examine how my actions contradicted my rhetoric. Crystal, one of the African American women in my group, was telling me how alienated she felt when I and the other guys mercilessly tromped on them. Then she added, "My anger at you subsided when I got to know the real person hiding inside your skin. When I saw your gentle side I felt differently about you." She was speaking of something that sounded mysterious to those who saw only my political face.

"What are you talking about, Raul's gentle side?" someone asked.

"We miss much about Raul when we only look at his strength and ignore his weakness," Crystal replied. "My view of Raul changed when I pushed to understand what really drives him, and he said his main agenda was 'to find the beauty in every person.' In that moment I knew he was a kindred spirit." Turning to me she said, "Raul, you are misguided in how you try to achieve your ends; if you just focused on finding the beauty in others, many more people would benefit. Please quit using proletariat slogans. A cause like 'finding the beauty in every person' is one I would join."

Crystal's statement was provocative. Then someone said, "Raul, what are you doing being a politician when you have a *poet* inside you?" That's when I knew what I had been hiding from, the missing part of me, the *fledgling poet* in me. In an instant I recognized that my soul had been crying out, nay screaming, for permission to give voice to its expressive side. Lying dormant in me and waiting to be found was the link that had been hiding, the *poet*. That's the part of my persona that can integrate and tie together the constructive and destructive versions of me.

As I continue, the Proletariat in me will fight to give voice to the people's concerns, the Politician in me will take his convictions to the people in the hope of sharing and building community, and the Poet in me will seek the beauty in what is around us. These three will journey together, finding their way jointly. This journey will never end but in the journey itself.

## *Dale: By the Rivers of Babylon*

Being a gay man has been agonizing. I hate having to stare each day into the face of AIDS and being forced to live according to outmoded models of maleness. I loved our life at the Farm, for there I was able to be fully me.

I entered the Out role with a vengeance and went quickly to a primal place. I began by going after the scalps of the Elites, making them the locus of a fury that arose from who knows where. I wanted the haves to be wounded and spent my time inventing ways to maim them. Then my anger boomeranged; the disdain I felt for them was really for the me that had always wanted to be an Elite in real life. I saw that I hate what I want to be, a paralyzing discovery, since I am unable to love what I currently am.

That's when I stopped attacking the Elites and focused on being what I was, an Out. Having to depend on the generosity of others was freeing. I've devoted much of my life to accumulating things and then protecting my useless possessions because I feared someone would take them from me. What a futile cycle. The things I work to acquire clutter my life but bring me no joy, filling my emptiness with more emptiness, and setting me on a search for more things. That's why having nothing was freeing. It stopped me from fearing that I would both lose what I have and lose myself in all that I have.

I was surprised by how easy it was to manipulate the other groups. We Outs decided to use our homelessness to guilt them into giving us what we wanted. Working out ways to make the Elites feel guilty was fun. I was a master at it. Someone asked me, "What guilt induction academy did you attend?" "I was born this way," I replied. "It was in the air I breathed in my family. It was so pervasive I never recognized it until now. Today I see that everything I do is propelled by guilt. Provoking guilt is how I get what I want." Acknowledging this really upset me.

Earlier in the semester I had let my guard down and directed my sexism and racism at Latania. This event was awful, but some good came from it. I was embarrassed. Some people were very upset, but Latania took it in stride. Her acceptance of me when I broke out of my shell and blurted out what common sense said to keep private helped so much. It led me to a resolution: to be honest with my fellow Outs no matter what trouble it created for them or me.

I opened my heart to them. This was what I told them. "A few years ago I became public about being gay. While that was hard, I was happy to be part of a community that would accept me. Then the AIDS epidemic struck with all its fury. As my friends got ill I became terrified. I had at last joined a community that would accept me, only to find that I might get killed for belonging to it. Had my new community been targeted by nature for extinction? A few months ago Gerald, my partner, discovered he had HIV. Of course, my first concern was if I did too. Mercifully I didn't. But so many of my friends did. The fears that came in the wake of Gerald's illness were exhausting. I was afraid I'd get infected. Also, why continue to invest in him knowing it would soon end and I would have to face suffering I could avoid if I walked away there and then. But what would that say about my integrity as a person if I left a man when he got ill? Yet I'm afraid that if I stay with him only because I cannot face myself for leaving him, the primary bond that ties us to each other will be guilt rather than love. I thought I loved Gerald, but now I am not sure. Could this bond be described as love if I want to walk away from it when it threatens me? But if I kill off my feelings for him and seek love elsewhere, will I be open to loving another since he too may have the virus? Or will I only let myself love someone who is not afflicted? What kind of love is it that declares the heart is open only to that which does not frighten it? Isn't it true that love only thrives when we are willing to be vulnerable?"

Telling others about my dilemmas was upsetting, but calming at the same time. I thought my burdens as a gay man were different from everyone else's, but we all had the same issues: we all ached to find a place where we felt we belonged, where life was ruled by love and not fear.

I felt completely at home at the Farm, even though we were supposedly the homeless. What made this experience magical was the level of acceptance we created. The key was being honest, to stop hiding from each other and ourselves. This was new for me. I made statement after statement that was contradictory. I spoke aloud my fears about my capacity to love. I laid out my guilt. I listed all the ways I felt like a fraud. I discussed my desire to be forgiven for all my intolerable flaws. It did not matter what I said or how I said it, the other Outs accepted me for what I am. They told me what they thought of my actions and my thoughts, but they never tried to take away my confusion or pain. Soon I was relating to myself differently, appreciating all I had rather than being upset by what I lacked. I loved finding the strength to tell everything to people not part of the gay and lesbian community. Becoming genuine with people who are not my people made them into my people; experiencing the love and acceptance of strangers has helped me not feel an alien to myself.

## *Crystal: Crowned with Garlands*

In the early part of this course the three American women of African descent were constantly being compared. Gloria and I were listened to and Latania was ignored. Initially it was subtle, but once we got real with one another I saw how much race dominated our interactions.

At one point, a white man said how he saw me. "Crystal, you are physically petite but have enormous presence. I am excited by your ideas, but your eyes are what draw me most. They exude such warmth. They also take in and see things the rest of us miss. You are unassuming but I've never met a person with the charisma and humility you have." I was flattered, but troubled. This same guy had said nothing when Dale made his bold and foolish statement about how his father "would never hire Latania as a secretary, although Gloria and Crystal would be acceptable."

The Dale-Latania exchange awakened in me something that refused to be put back to sleep. Initially I was furious at Dale. We were friends and I felt betrayed by him and angry at myself for being so gullible to think he was beyond that kind of racism. But what lit my fuse was Dale's description of our employment prospects in his father's business. If he was hiring a secretary, Gloria or I would get the job. It distressed me that Dale used the position of a secretary to make his point. Was this the only job his father would give a black woman? All of us were about to get prestigious graduate degrees, making us as qualified as Dale, yet he still thought of us as secretaries.

Suddenly it was clear. As black women, we would always be seen as candidates for subservient positions, no matter what our credentials were. I had dared to believe that my education would let me compete at the highest levels as an equal. Not if people like Dale were doing the hiring! He saw me only as a potential secretary! When Dale used me and Gloria to degrade another black woman I thought, "Oh no, the master is up to his old tricks with his proverbial house negro versus field negro scenario." Although the house negro was treated a little better than the field negro, both were despised and pitted against each other. I was insulted and demeaned that the quasi-acceptance I received was because Dale saw me as tame, like a house negro, and used this to wound another black woman who chose not to adapt to his standards.

I was surprised how well Latania handled this. She was so composed. She understood that what Dale said was about him and not her. However, it was also about me. Others were concerned because he had demeaned Latania, but he demeaned me too! I hate being acceptable to such people! It showed me the things I do so whites will feel at ease. Do the Dales of the world have the right to be comfortable, while giving safe haven to such attitudes?

Later, like Latania, I felt grateful to Dale for his honesty, even though I hated what he had said. His speaking the awful truth highlighted the energy I waste when I try to conform to others' expectations in the hope of gaining their favor. As I accepted I could not change the Dales in my life, I let go of trying to do this again. This set me on a new and exciting path. I started by going back to my own African American roots. There I rediscovered our collective strength that sustained my people through the ages. The words of W. E. B. Du Bois helped me. "One ever feels his twoness, an American, a negro: two souls, two thoughts, two unreconciled strivings; two warring ideals in one dark body, whose dogged strength alone keeps it from being torn asunder."[19] Du Bois was my companion. Together we felt the dilemma captured by Faust: "Two souls, alas, within me dwell."

For days I thought about how my people are seen as suffering from both paranoia and multiple personality disorder. These come from our endless questioning of whether we are rejected because we don't have the experience and skills or because of who we are. We can never answer this, but we are also never free of it. I had felt my inner fragmentation since childhood, and by my teens I knew that many of the tensions in me were a product of the divided world in which I live. However, I had convinced myself that the evils of racism could thrive only in the world of the ignorant, that it did not exist among the educated. Dale's outburst ended this illusion. As this belief crumbled, I saw how my inner fragmentation had been heightened by this false assumption.

Dale had shown me the myth I had bought into. My years at Andover, Stanford, and Wharton offered no escape from the racism and sexism poisoning us or from Du Bois's and Faust's "Two souls, alas, within me dwell." The misconception that had ruled my life was shattered, bringing both an immense sadness and much needed liberation.

By the time I arrived at the Farm, I had decided I would accept whatever position I was born into and strive to just be myself. I would not try to change a thing, but would spend all my energies focusing on the forces around me that normally mask my inner self, throw me off, and leave me feeling alienated. I hoped to refind my inner self and learn how to remain connected with that self no matter what was going on. As a Middle I was caught between the Elites and the Outs, but I aligned myself with neither. Instead I tried to remain true to my Self, wherever I was. There were times I wanted to change things, but I just let everything be. I tried not to shut others out or to connect with them. I just let my estrangement exist. There were times when I wanted to relieve others' pain, but I took no action and instead just empathized with their hurt.

At every anguished turn I tried to wrap my arms around myself in a loving embrace and, when that was impossible, to note what made it difficult. At the Farm, as I grew more connected to my inner self, surprisingly this increased my connectedness to everything and everyone around me. I made it a moment-by-moment discipline to let go of any thought that made me feel fragmented.

I regularly went for long walks alone, picking up on an old affirmation of Nietzsche's that "no idea is true unless it is thought in the open air" and Gandhi's reminder that "to grow spiritually you must walk." Being alone in the open was great therapy. There, in the woods, I wept many of the tears of my yesteryears. Although I may appear together, I had been quite fragmented. The frightened child who left home at thirteen to go to boarding school and then college in the hope of escaping the ills of the city was still with me, as were my adolescent feelings of inadequacy and of wanting to be treated as an equal. I had yet to find a place where I felt valued and accepted for who I really am.

During the review I listened in awe to the experiences of my fellow sojourners, most of whom I had never imagined could become my kindred spirits. What they said touched me in ways I would not have expected, Dale included. I saw myself in everyone's struggles, which helped me acknowledge that I too have felt *not at home* in my spirit or in my world. Accepting this truth from which I had been hiding helped me grow more at peace, and has shown me a clearer sense of what I must do to become internally integrated.

I loved learning that people who felt alienated from one another shared so much common ground. I, for one, had never stopped to think that the privileged white males I have encountered might feel no more at home with themselves or the world around them than I did. I had presumed that being a Caucasian male guaranteed them acceptance and freedoms I would never know. In the deep places in the soul, where it really matters, this is not the case.

During the weeks we shared together I abandoned some outmoded self-images and learned to believe in myself and others in a new way. And I started to draw upon lessons that my people learned though the anguish of slavery about how to keep the creative and suffering selves connected. With that sense of self in place, it became impossible to hate and easy to see every adversary as an ally, as a person just like myself, struggling to be whole in a frightening world.

## Waiting All the Day Long

The stories of Raul, Dale, and Crystal touched on many themes that resonated with my own experience, particularly the part of me that spent more than three decades hiding emotionally. Like them, I had spent many years hoping to be emancipated from something; exactly what was not clear until it occurred. We all yearned for acceptance and thought it was the approval of others we needed. What a surprise to learn that the deprivations, which accumulated as a consequence of hoping for others' acceptance, vanished when the abundance already residing in the self was released. It emerged when the accepting self ceased to be dwarfed by the conflicts between the parts of the self trying to construct a life and the portion feeling crushed by life.

Raul and Crystal were eloquent about their searching: for Raul it was to locate and give voice to the expressive, what he called the poet; for Crystal it was to access the third soul, one capable of accepting that "within me two souls do dwell."

As I took in Dale's experiences I thought about other gays and lesbians who still struggled for acceptance. Luke, a man in his early thirties, was very much in my mind. He had once written, "Since my early teens I've been tormented because I'm gay. This is a dilemma because I've been taught that homosexuality contradicts God's laws. I was born into a strict family and a fundamentalist church. For years I tried to not be gay, but how do you not be what you are! Over and over I've dated women, feigning my interest in them. It always turns out the same way. I keep trying because I want to marry and have children, values espoused by my church and my family, the two most important parts of my life. But I can't continue being a fraud. I have devoured many books on the subject, spent endless hours poring over the scriptures, prayed, and talked with church counselors. I've tried to suppress my feelings, but that did not work. I've tried to imagine coming out but I can't do that either; to accept homosexuality would mean giving up every dream I've had.

"The seeds of low self-esteem and self-hatred were planted in me early by my church, my family, and the society. I removed myself emotionally to keep my feelings hidden. I hate myself for this deception, but I equally hate trying to deny my nature. I cannot accept that this is my lot in life, yet I am paralyzed. I have no more control over this than I have over the color of my eyes! I'm at an impasse. Each side of me screams for a resolution, but each also demands it not be sacrificed in my search for a solution. I see my choices as celibacy or accepting my gayness. I could have a life without sex, but to forego love and romance would be like letting go of life itself. But to have the assurance of God's love, I must be straight. A civil war rages within me. I don't know what to do."

I was touched by Luke's plight. His faith and his humanity were on a collision course. What would emerge from the ashes of this inevitable crash? Would Luke surface with his humanity intact and still have a keen sense of the divine? The most plaintive aspect of Luke's bind was his belief that both God and his family would not love him if he failed to make himself acceptable to them. I understood Luke's doubts, having lived my own version of this. While my wrestling had been around different issues, I too had to learn that God was not limited to the Sunday School boxes I had used to contain Her, that my mind was too limited to grasp what was in the heart of the Almighty, and that the beliefs passed on to me were only a scaffold to house my faith and were not to be confused with the substance of faith itself.

I thought of some of the great characters of history that had been in binds just as intense as Luke's. I wondered what was in Martin Luther's heart as he grew alienated from the church he loved, what a lifetime of fighting the slave trade in Great Britain had done to William Wilberforce, what Gandhi thought as he recognized the scourge of colonialism, what Rosa Parks felt as she pondered sitting in the "white only" section of the bus. I wondered if this anguish Luke was going through was preparing him to liberate others along with himself. What would the Martin Luther in him suggest he do? What would the William Wilberforce in him advise? What would the Gandhi in him inspire? What would the Rosa Parks in him advocate? What gifts would Luke bring to humanity as he tried to find a path with heart?

While thinking about Dale and Luke, another man came to mind. Brad had been a student in a course I taught many years ago. One assignment in this class was to observe a group of people going through major changes. Brad, a twenty-year-old, had joined two other gays and two lesbians, and they formed a group themselves. Their project was to study themselves as they garnered the inner resources needed to come out in a place where it was difficult to be public about being homosexual. Brad decided he wanted to tell his parents face to face that he was gay and to use this class as a forum to come out for the first time. Toward the end of the semester, Brad stood up in class one day and with a trembling voice made the following statements.

"Today, I am making my first public acknowledgment that I am gay. Getting to this point has been wild. I decided I must tell my parents first. I did that this past weekend. My parents are great people, but I was afraid they'd stop loving me once they knew I am gay. I called them on Thursday and told them I would be home on the weekend. They were surprised, because I never go home in the weeks leading into exams. They knew something was up. So I blurted it out and got off the phone as quickly as possible. I said, "I know you are going to be very upset with me, but I want to tell you something I've kept secret for too long. I can't do that any more. I'm just going to tell you now and then we can talk about it on Saturday. I am gay!"

"Neither of them said a thing for minutes. I could hear my mother crying, and then my dad signed off by saying, 'We'll see you on the weekend, son.' That was that; I had told them!

"I was terrified going home. I readied myself to be thrown out. When I arrived my mom tried to hug me, but we were both stiff. Dad shook my hand. He never does that. We went into the library, the place where all serious conversations in my family take place. I was petrified.

"My dad spoke first. 'After you called on Thursday we were in shock. Brad, we had no idea! We were sure you had undergone a breakdown and were convinced that you needed psychiatric help. We thought of this as something needing to be fixed, so on Friday we scheduled you for a summer of therapy with the best psychiatrist in town. Last night we came to our senses and realized that it is not you who needs help, but us. We are the ones with the problem! You have been learning for years how to accept yourself for what you are. Your telling us is a mark that you have reached a level of self-acceptance few achieve. We admire you for the courage that must have taken. Now it is our job to mature to the same level. We don't know how to do this, so instead of sending you to the psychiatrist, we've decided to go ourselves. Being father to you and your sister has been the most significant thing in my life, and I want to do nothing to jeopardize that.'

"By the time my dad had finished all three of us were in tears, and the hug my mother gave me was like nothing I've got before. I can't begin to tell you how it felt. I just said, 'I always knew you loved me, but now I really know it!' "

This was a poignant moment for all hundred students in this class. I felt joy for Brad, for the acceptance he received from his parents. Brad had learned something that was yet ahead for me. My return to China was five years hence, and my grace moment was still in the making.

•

After the revolution of 1949 the Chinese were allowed no contact with the rest of the world. All mail to the West was banned. Any letter to or from China was opened and censored. The mere act of receiving mail from the West was viewed as political subversion and evoked harsh penalties. For thirty years my parents had no contact with some of their best friends in life. For Dad, this was the emotional equivalent of having his leg amputated.

Then came "the letter." It released tides of emotion. Its path was quite circuitous. For more than a decade, Cephus — that was our name for him; Hsun-Keng Wang was his Chinese name — had tried to find out what happened to my dad. He knew nothing of my father's whereabouts. Cephus presumed that if we got out of China alive, my family would go to Australia. He wrote many letters, smuggling them out of China one way or another. None of them reached my parents. Then one day in the late 1970s, a note with only a few lines came via a doctor visiting Melbourne for a conference. A tight network of Chinese contacts had worked for years to track my dad down.

My father was so relieved that Cephus was alive. The first note to reach him was very brief and everything was in code: Cephus simply stated that he believed a man by the name of Gordon Smith could locate an obscure medical journal and would be willing to order a copy of it for his hospital. This was the way we discovered his address, but it also gave us subtle cues about how to communicate without jeopardizing Cephus politically. Dad called me in the United States and asked me to find the journal and send it to Cephus.

We were subsequently to learn how Cephus and his wife, Judy, survived the many turmoils of Chinese life, and how for three decades they had hoped to meet up again with my parents, despite the fact that the politics of the day still made this impossible. Cephus was a physician, trained in both Western and traditional medicines, who had suffered greatly after the revolution of 1949. Because he and my dad were such good friends, Cephus was deemed "an enemy of the revolution" and forced to spend years as a farm hand in a rural work camp, the Chinese equivalent of Siberia. When the political winds shifted with the Great Leap Forward in 1958, Cephus was reinstated and brought back into the medical world to practice his profession. This lasted ten years, but in the late 1960s he was again scapegoated. He was assigned to clean out latrines, except for the occasional emergency call to operate on a dignitary, when no other surgeon of his caliber was available.

By the time of our visit in 1984, Cephus had been back in the mainstream for a while. He was superintendent of a hospital and was professor of surgery at the local medical school. He was also a ranking member of the communist party and had managed to take his place in the political drama of his day without renouncing what he valued most.

We had designed our 1984 return to China so it would culminate in a reunion with Cephus and Judy. We all planned to converge on Shanghai, the city where my parents had married forty-four years earlier. For more than two weeks my father, brother, and I had been having a grand time. But my dad's psychological and medical collapse on our last day in Chengdu and during the two days we were in Xian threatened the one thing

Dad wanted most in life, the chance to see Cephus again. This was the prime reason we were reluctant to abort our trip and air ambulance him out. However, there seemed little alternative. So once we were in Beijing we started the process. It was a tough judgment call. We had decided I was the one to escort Dad in the air ambulance to Australia. My brother would go ahead to Shanghai and meet with Cephus and Judy.

Soon after arriving in Beijing, Dad's distress began to subside a little. We decided to hold off leaving for half a day and see what happened. Dad did not get any better, but he was also no worse. The best advice said to let him rest and see what unfolded. Through all this I was trying to be a responsible son. We were so upset that Dad might have to leave before this long-anticipated reunion with Cephus and Judy. These old friends had dreamed about this gathering for three decades, and to be this close and not have it happen due to illness was just too much to bear!

Fortunately Dad was able to hang on, and he subsequently recovered sufficiently for us to continue our journey. As his health improved, we understood how much Dad's physical collapse had been a bodily expression of his reliving the terror of 1949. He had looked into the jaws of the beast from which he had been fleeing all his life and actually survived. Putting himself back together again was not going to be easy, but he was an old man and it so happened that touching his ancient terror had been a life imperative.

As Dad's symptoms subsided and my own anxiety lessened, I began to piece together the fragments of information I'd gleaned from him over the previous few days and added them to what had emerged over the past two decades. I entered the mystery via a different angle. Why had Dad been so afraid? I decided to assume he was guilty and not innocent, as he had always claimed, and to see what he might have done to incur such political wrath. In the next forty-eight hours the picture became clear. Dad was not a CIA agent, but the CIA craftily used him. So it was reasonable that the Chinese had assumed he was a spy and an enemy of the people. This was the story:

In the 1930s Mao Dedong, a man my father used to call the "bandit," along with his gangs of robbers, made aggressive forays into the villages, robbing them of all available food and destabilizing life for all.[20] The peasants were in a perpetual state of terror as these armed plunderers struck without warning. It was their intent to weaken the nation, and they succeeded.

As the control of the country began to slip out of the Nationalist government's hands, huge sums of foreign money from the West were pumped into China and laundered via the churches, missionaries, and anyone else who could be used as a conduit. Dad was treasurer of one of the major missions, and he had been the handler of a large portion of this foreign money.

In the late 1930s, during the Depression in the West, the Chinese economy was on the verge of collapsing. Chiang Kai-shek, who a decade later was driven off the mainland and who moved his operation to Taiwan, was militarily trying to hold off Mao Dedong and his gangs. Today we'd call them terrorists. As that military government struggled to hold China's economy together, the communists were counting on the collapse of that very economy to fuel their own populism.

The communist revolution was on the verge of making a huge advance when World War II broke out. America wanted to avoid a full-blown civil war in China during the period of Japanese expansion, since it believed that a weakened neighbor on Japan's border would fuel their aggression. So the United States brokered a secret deal. They convinced the Nationalists and Communists to place their conflict on hold and fight side by side against Japan. Then, when the war was over, they could resume their domestic battle, with the starting point being exactly where they had left off at the time the deal was made. In return for agreeing to this pact, the United States fully armed both the Communists and the Nationalists, assuming these weapons would be used against the Japanese.

China's internal battle was frozen in place, to be recommenced when World War II ended. However, Mao stockpiled a large portion of the munitions provided by the United States. Hence, the Communists were well armed when Japan surrendered. Ironically, Mao's victory a few years later was made possible because of the weapons the United States had given to the Communists!

The quick rise of the Communists distressed the United States, who wanted Chiang Kai-shek and the Nationalists to remain in power. They poured a fortune into China between 1945 and 1949. Much of it was under-the-table money.

My dad was involved in the foreign propping up of the government opposed to communism. One way the United States got money into China was by buying Chinese products at highly inflated prices, shipping them to Hong Kong, and then selling them at a fraction of the purchase price. In this way large sums of money were put into the economy via business deals. To enable this to work, two foreign exchange rates were established, one publicly sanctioned by the government and another informal, black market rate. The Chinese Nationalist government, very dependent on the economic benefits of having a black market, encouraged it and fully supported it. However, the Nationalists had to act as if they did not agree to it. Of course, the negotiations to establish this under-the-table monetary exchange system, and the government's collusion in this process, were kept highly secret. My dad was one of three Westerners who set this black market rate.

From my dad's point of view, he did this because he was asked to by the mission. It was a way to get rice at a cheap price and make available more food for the poor and the starving. However, the mission made it clear to him that the actions he was taking, as their representative, would be viewed as illegal. If he was ever caught they would deny their involvement and he would be made the fall guy. Dad actually acknowledged to me for the first time, while we were in Xian, that he found out he had been set up by the mission when he realized the minutes of the meeting in which this was decided made no mention of the decision to have Gordon Smith act on the mission's behalf as one of setters of the black market rate. He tried to get them to insert corrections in the minutes, but the mission authorities refused. He had been caught in a bind from which he could not escape. He was set up to be their scapegoat. From all the information I gathered, nothing pointed to his having any larger political involvement than this.

This helped to explain everything. Dad had given so much to China and was deeply invested in his mission work. However, after returning to Australia, with one exception in 1950, he never made a public statement on religious issues again. He worked as an accountant doing tax returns for families and small businesses. His faith remained important to him, but as I grew up and doubts of all kinds reigned in my blossoming mind and heart, Dad never said a word of what he thought about anything of import.

While we were in Beijing Dad rested peacefully. The bodily symptoms attending his emotional collapse began to lessen, and it was possible for us to continue on to Shanghai, where we were to meet up with Cephus and Judy. Despite his sickness and the depression that was linked to his paranoia and his Parkinson's, as we arrived in Shanghai Dad's excitement was sky-high.

However, something strange occurred when Gordon and Cephus met that caught my brother and me by surprise. We had decided to let these old friends be alone together for the first couple of hours, figuring they would value the privacy. So we got Dad out of his sick bed, propped him up in a comfortable chair, and slipped out just before Cephus and Judy arrived.

We returned two hours later to a room completely devoid of energy. The three of them were looking at each other and saying nothing. A pall of depression filled the space. After a round of greetings and some conversation with no substance, Cephus rose, shook hands with us and indicated they had to leave. He asked if they could come to the train station to say goodbye to us two days later when we were to leave Shanghai.

My heart almost caved in. We had all scheduled forty-eight hours to be together, and the reunion seemed to have collapsed before it was even off the ground. I sensed we were in some cultural cul-de-sac. Later, my brother and I realized we had made a dreadful mistake electing to be absent the initial moment when Dad met with Cephus and Judy. We weren't thinking, and Dad was not well enough to catch this. In Chinese tradition a gathering of this kind was about two families coming together, not about two old men who had once been buddies hanging out. So when Gordon's sons were not present, this was seen as disrespectful of Cephus and his family and sent the message that our father had no standing in our family at all. The irreverence of the sons was such a huge slight that Cephus, Judy, and Gordon were paralyzed by it. No amount of deep conversation, or small talk, was even possible when placed under a canopy of humiliation this large.

I refused to let it all go, however. I immediately said, "No, no, no! We must have a meal together. Let me arrange lunch for us all." That broke the ice. You can't sit and break bread — actually share rice is the more apt metaphor in China — if there is no mutual respect. Within a few minutes, by our words, our actions, and our demeanor, we managed to undo our cultural faux pas. The emotional mood changed and both families excitedly spent every waking moment with each other for the next two days.

Cephus obviously had very deep affection for my father. When we were together the only thing that mattered was their friendship. Never mind that their ties to each other had cost Cephus dearly, including many years in political disgrace. He had refused to renounce my dad just to get out of trouble. None of that mattered to him, nor did he hold any apparent bitterness over the way his life had unfolded. His body might have been scarred by these historical events, but his spirit certainly was not.

Their time together was remarkable, but the details are not relevant here. The reason for this piece of the history is to set the stage for what happened to me. We were all sitting around the meal table telling stories. Judy, Cephus's wife, now an old but very beautiful Chinese woman, was regaling my brother and me with reports about what we had been like as children. I had no clear memory of her as a person. But oh, how she remembered us! She filled our mealtimes with wonderful tales. She was charming and enchanting. Being with both Cephus and Judy and getting a first-hand account of what life had been like for the communist Chinese was very educative and extremely touching.

It is worth reporting that the dominant message I received during my youth in Australia was that the Chinese communists were the enemy. They had tried to kill us when I was five and, if given a chance, would dominate the whole world, subjugating every political system to their needs. Yet in this land of my early childhood I was feeling enveloped by such immense acceptance and love I had no wish to ever leave.

Suddenly, out of the blue, Judy looked me right in the eye and asked me a question I never expected to hear: "Do you remember how you would ask me to carry you?"

I didn't! I was surprised by her question and immediately curious, given my history with "being carried" and the anguish of my encounter with my dad in Bombay. I asked her to say more.

"You would often say to me, 'Judy, I'm tired, please carry me.' Sometimes it was when we were all out together. Other times it was just to get you up the stairs into your bedroom when we were visiting at night."

I could not contain myself and blurted out, "And Judy, did you carry me?"

She looked deeply into my eyes and replied without a moment's hesitation and with boundless emotion, "Oh, Kenwyn, I *loved* to carry you! I loved to carry *you!* I loved to *carry* you!"

My heart just melted. For a moment all of time stood still. When it recommenced, the whole of my inner landscape had changed. It has never been the same since.

I had lived all of my life feeling that no one was willing to carry me. Then I learned how wrong I was. In a country we thought of as our enemy was a little old Chinese lady, the spouse of my father's best friend in life, who for thirty-five years remembered how much she loved to carry a little boy by the name of Kenwyn Kingsford Smith!

In that moment the wound that had once been the source of such festering pain for me became a wellspring of inner joy. And it remains that way to this day. In an instant I moved from experiencing myself as a wounded soul to a person who was blessed. I saw clearly how this emotional injury of long ago had become a fertile field in which had been planted the seeds of Grace. Much of my life journey had been preparing me to collect that blessing.

To receive that gift required me to meet up again with a beautiful old lady who had faithfully carried me in her heart for three and a half decades. Through all the travails of her own life, Judy had kept that precious key that someday was to unlock the mystery defining my life. What is even more amazing is that she was one of "the enemies." She lived on the other side of the world, in a country closed to the West, in a place against which we were always poised to go to war.

At the first opportunity, I went to be alone. That's when the tears came. I cried in a way I had never done before. For the first time in my experience, each teardrop seemed to contain within it total sadness and total joy.

Those tears not only gave my emotions a much-needed bath; they baptized my spirit. After an hour of crying it was all over. Since that moment, everything has felt different in ways I can hardly state. I now know why the hymn writer coined the term "Amazing Grace" and what is meant by the ancient psalmist's words, "Even in the presence of my enemies, Thou hast prepared a feast for me."

*I will celebrate thy love when morning comes.*

Psalm 59:16

# Chapter 10

# *Dying to Live*

It was heartwarming and uplifting to be with these young men and women as they reflected on their attempts to find a place in the world, especially as they realized how each advance also set them back. They were all sure to buy homes, work and live in organizations and communities with resources, and be among the influential members of their generation. Yet their paths were leading them further away from the *sense of home* they craved. Their experiences at the Lab had invited them to treat the vulnerable heart as fertile soil in which the truths of the ages had been planted long ago.

What makes a community or an organization into a wholesome place? For a human system to be whole, the part with the *power to construct* and the part with the *power to destroy* need to be linked. The connections binding these extremes enable the center to hold. If the middle crumbles, disintegration is near by. For a system to provide a communal home for all its members, it must have strong mediating and integrating processes. What does it take to be *at home* with the self? This requires the bringing together of our creative and our suffering selves, parts of each human being that are located at opposite sides of a ravine that can only be connected by the accepting self.

## *A Healing Cancer*

These insights from the Lab at Fellowship Farm still left something critical unexplored. As I wept and laughed and celebrated with all the participants, I was thinking about a defining event of my own life, the death of my mother. As these young people were grasping at life, I was reflecting on death. While this seemed strange, it made sense because it was my mother's dying that helped me understand why, all my days, I had felt not at home in this world.

The understandings I gleaned through my mother's dying led me to no longer fight this feeling. Today I wrap my arms around it and celebrate it. As I do this I feel increasingly at home within myself; I find that I belong in more and more organizations and communities; and I am increasingly delighted by the life I have been given, even when surrounded by conflicts that at times are quite unmanageable.

Although I had such difficulty with her emotional detachment during all the years of her mothering, it was my mum's forthrightness in death that taught me about one of the mysteries of my life. It was as if she brought to her dying all the passion, all the insight, and all the enchantment that she had not expended during her seventy-eight years. When I think that this woman, who first gave me life and then dampened much of that life during my growing years, could offer such a reconciling gift as she went to her grave, it leaves me amazed.

It all came suddenly. Our twin sons had been born the year before, and we had spent three of their first twelve months in Australia. During our time with the larger family, my mother was in the fullness of her life, making grandmothering and her artwork the centerpieces of her days. A week after we left, she became ill. A month later she had surgery. There were mild signs of cancer, but the doctors expected she would recover fully. However, she began losing weight, and all was not well. Further investigation showed the cancer had spread to the liver.

When she called to tell me this, I was taken aback, but, without thinking, blurted out, "I guess it's dying time, Mother." She responded with a deep sigh and said, "Yes, it seems like it is!" And we wept together on the phone. I dropped everything and went to be with her. We decided to keep her at home. There would be no hospitals, tubes, or last-minute heroics, just gentle medication to limit pain. I was there for eight days as caretaker of both her and my dad, whose continuing decline meant he too needed constant attention. Then my siblings took over until the end.

Those days getting ready for death were the most significant of my relationship with my mother. She was very ill and exceedingly frail, yet I had never seen her looking so healthy. Her body was fading quickly, but as this happened her spirit became clearer and clearer. Something remarkable was taking place before my eyes. She was becoming whole in a way I had never seen in any person before. Mother was being healed, not in the physical sense, but in a form that went beyond the body. This gave me a new appreciation of the term "healing," a derivative of the Greek word *holos*, which means whole. As mother became more ill, she was becoming more *whole*.

Just before I arrived, she had moved to a Zen-like acceptance that she was about to die. On the first day she could still walk, but by the time I left, she needed a great deal of help simply to move. Within twenty-four hours of my departure she took to her bed and never got up again. She died a few days later.

Being with her as she prepared to pass from this life was exhilarating, even though it was torturous watching her age several years each day, as her body became that of a hundred-year-old. I was startled at the beginning because she was so gaunt, having lost sixty pounds in the weeks since I had seen her. I could not get used to the image of her as a mere silhouette. After a few hours of feeling awkward about her visible decline, I told her what a shock it was to see her fade so quickly.

That broke the ice, and we started talking about what it was like to be dying. Mother was ready to move on and had a serenity that was simultaneously calming and disarming. She was withdrawing from life with a quiet dignity. Nothing of a material nature had meaning for her any more, not even food. While she was pleased to hear the things I told her about my life and my family, she had no energy to ask questions. Her focus had turned inward. The outside was becoming irrelevant. Despite the obvious torment of her body she was startlingly at peace. I was curious about the source of her tranquility, so I asked her. She said it was easy because she was now able to live entirely in the present. For her the past was complete, and there was nothing left to struggle over.

We spoke about how she felt about dying before my dad, since we all had assumed she would be there to care for him in his waning years. For more than a decade she had kept life going for them both, and it was impossible to imagine his coping without her. She laughed. "I always thought it was my job to look after him, but I guess that's not to be. It is strange because your father has been ready to die for so long, whereas I've not been prepared. It will work out though. He must have something still to do that he can't accomplish while I'm around. He'll find his own way."

I loved my mother's matter-of-fact manner. I had never heard her be this direct, this straightforward, this clear. Every few hours we would have a fifteen-minute conversation. That was all she could sustain before needing rest. In between I went about the chores of caring for a home and helping my father cope with the physical and emotional demands of his own shrinking capacities. He understood that his lifelong partner was dying, but had limited energy to deal with it. He was happy to have others around assisting with this transition.

Constantly running through my mind throughout these days was the music of Dvorak's Symphony no. 9, *From the New World,* especially the sequence that has the motif of an old Negro spiritual, "Goin' home, goin' home, Lord, I'm goin' home." I was humming it to myself all the time. This tune conveys a soul-filled longing that touches the deepest places in the heart. "Goin' home, goin' home, Lord, I'm goin' home." This seemed fitting, for mother was clearly on her pilgrimage home. England! China! Australia! These were but wayside stops on her journey, sanctuaries along the path.

## The Isolated Hut in the Bush

I also thought often about a gift Mother once sent me, a landscape that she painted in her sixties, just as her artist's eye was coming to life.[21] The painting is of an old weatherbeaten hut totally enveloped by a storm-ridden sky. One's looking is drawn initially to clouds conveying a sense of the ominous. Right at the point when the dark and threatening sky is about to close in on you, the eye is pulled to the center of the painting where the old hut radiates isolation and loneliness. It is a compelling place so one wants to move in and make it home, yet it contains an overpowering feeling of desolation, and one also wants to leave right away. Moving to the foreground, where there is a blaze of fiery colors in endless celebration, it is possible to gain relief from these opposing emotions. Here the richness, confidence, vitality, and assurance replenish what the storm and the lonely hut depleted.

When mother first sent me this painting I saw it as a summary of a universal message: adversity guides us to those intensely alone places where we are invited to find the courage to face all that torments us. She had made a similar, though more delicate, statement in a letter when I was deep in the doldrums: "Affliction helps us keep our values right, and then we are able to enjoy the better things of life in a more enlightened way." However, the message of this painting was much bolder than that gentle maternal entreatment. It contained a brutal forthrightness, what Martin Luther King captured in his proclamation, "Every symphony of hope is sculpted from the rock of despair." That painting has hung for years above the fireplace in our living room, nourishing me each day and drawing the silent reflection of those who enter our abode.

Until this time, I had viewed this treasure as my mother's special gift to me. However, as I rifled though the paintings stashed under the beds we had slept in as children, I found many with the same theme. Then I recognized that this painting was a metaphor for her whole life. She recorded this on canvas on a regular basis, like a ritual recentering, to remind her of the conviction she used to guide her though life: "In my alone place is housed the strength I need to weather life's threatening storms, so long as I remain focused on the celebration of color, of light, of all that is ahead of me." This painting represented the story of her life, during which she had asked endlessly, "What and where is home?" Mother was now preparing herself to learn the answers to these ageless questions as she readied herself for death.

It turned out that she lived the bulk of her days in foreign lands: sixteen years in China and forty in Australia. She did not complain about this, yet she never ceased to be an Englishwoman at heart. Her letters at different times conveyed this. Anticipating her visit to England in 1972, for the first time since World War II, she commented, "It's going to be strange to go home, with no home as I've known it. There will be many a lump in my throat as I walk over familiar ground and think of the past." Then a week after arriving she wrote, "Since I have been here I have relived a lifetime. It has been a happy week, and also a sad one. Sometimes I have been with old friends and we have laughed until the tears have rolled down our faces, and other times we have been swallowing our sadness. Joy and sorrow interwoven — this is life — one balancing the other. Oh, how I have missed my friends of long standing, those who knew my beginning, to whom no explanation is necessary."

She experienced great joy visiting her birthplace and the scenes of her childhood. She wrote as follows: "And then there are those lovely leafy lanes of Warwickshire. I've seen the woods where, as children, we picked bluebells, buttercups, cowslips, and primroses, and where we sat in the fields and made daisy chains. Surely there is a little bit of heaven here. It is hard to leave."

As the days slipped by Mother and I spoke of everything of import. One morning when I asked how she was, instead of giving me a comment about her body, as was her custom, she said something I never expected. "In a strange way I feel really excited."

"About what?" I asked.

"About dying!"

Responding to my astonishment, she continued, "I feel like I am on the verge of the biggest adventure of my life. I don't know what is ahead. They call it *dying,* but it feels more like a *birth.* I am excited. Everything will be new in ways I can't even imagine. I hope it won't be long now."

This began a wonderful conversation. Mother had come to the realization that death was not an end to anything, but a beginning so great and so vast that the human mind could simply not imagine it. She was convinced that her time on this earth had been but a prelude, that life as we know it is not the symphony, but the announcement about the festival to come.

What a wonderful thought: dying is like a birth! The confidence that mother radiated that day altered how I understood what home is. It invited me to see death as merely an entree to a celebration we cannot comprehend. While I had understood this as an essential teaching of the sacred literatures, it had always felt abstract. Having it come from my own mother, especially given the difficulties of our relationship over the years, made it real and tangible. Death is like a birth! What a soul-restoring image!

## Be Like the Bird

When it was finally time for us to say our lifetime goodbyes, which we had been doing incrementally over the previous few days, it was a moment with few words. We just hugged and wept as the taxi waited outside to take me to the airport for the long flight from Australia to the United States. There was precious little left of her frail body to hug. However, her robust spirit wrapped me in her warm embrace. Her tears were strong and everything about her being was inspiring. There was just one last thing I had to say to her.

Many years earlier, in response to my telling her about a series of troublesome events in my life, she had sent me a letter consisting of a few words by Victor Hugo. At the time she seemed to be gently exhorting me to recognize that I already had within me the resources I needed to climb out of the despair that held me in its grip. This had helped greatly, because I had been looking everywhere but within to find the healing I craved. That day, those words of Victor Hugo's became indelibly etched on my mind and have sustained me many times over the years.[22]

Through the tears, my choking voice, and the intense longing of a distressed child I said my goodbye, quoting back to her the lines of Victor Hugo she'd once given me. "Mother, as you go, 'be like the bird, that pausing in her flight awhile on boughs too slight, feels them give way beneath her and yet sings, knowing that she hath wings.' Be like the bird, Mum. And thanks for singing your song, and for teaching me that I am to sing mine also."

She touched my face with her frail fingers and the tender palpation of a mother's love enveloped me. All of time stood still as I was wrapped in the arms of eternity. I wanted to stay in that moment forever. As I wrenched myself away and waved my last farewell, she just smiled, her face awash with the tears of the ages; I walked off with every fiber of my being knowing that heaven was very near.

While I knew it would not be long before mother died, the doctors said it could be a few days or a few weeks. I settled back into my life in the United States with Sara and our infant twins. However, without warning, my mother's spirit made one last visit to me. One night, as I was on the verge of falling asleep half a world away, I suddenly felt her in the room with me. I sat bolt upright. Her presence was gentle but unmistakable. It only lasted a moment. She lovingly greeted me with the gentlest assurance that, although we would never see each other again in this form, we would always be together. Then she was gone.

I knew she had died in that moment. I got up to await the call from my dad and to be quietly with my spirit. At dawn all of life would bustle with details: international flights, burial plots, services, etc. I wanted to be with my thoughts of Mother, to ponder her passing, and to let the tears of sad gladness bathe my spirit. A few hours later Dad called and confirmed that the moment of my mother's visitation in my bedroom was the exact time of her death.

*Death is like a birth.* Mother had just gone home. In the stillness of the night, with the dull sounds of my family's slumber in the background, I came to understand that I had never felt at home, *because this existence is not my home.* This feeling of homelessness that had troubled me for so long was not an illusion to be dismantled but a reality to be accepted. Home is not to be found in this mortal existence. It is a condition of the spirit. It is a characteristic of the state we can all reach some day and to which our earthly lives constantly point.

In the quiet, it was clear to me why I had been so confused. I had been looking for home in the wrong place. In fact it was my very looking that was distracting me. If I would but let myself fall into the realities of all the ways I felt I did not fit in, I would be in much closer contact with my spirit, both the home within and the home beyond.

Six years later my father died. In contrast to my mother's death, his was very drawn out. It was hard to imagine why he was lingering. Each year, more and more of him faded away, and by the end there was little of him left. His brain seemed to have only the capacity of an infant, and he required constant care. The last time I saw him he had only a hazy recollection of who I was and even that was dreamlike and fleeting. That was hard, but I was grateful we had said all we needed to while he was in the fullness of his life.

At the end, his body was nothing but bone with a thin covering of skin stretched across it. For the last many weeks he did not have the strength to move. His Parkinson's, mixed with the effects of aging, had advanced him to the point where he seemed to be in a state of perpetual rigor mortis. While it was painful to witness his decline, something important was obviously happening. He had lived such a troubled life; it was hard to picture him not being in anguish at death. However, as he approached the end he entered a peaceful state. Mother had been right. There were some things Dad had to do before he could die.

My sister was with my dad during the last few days. His voice was gone, the only words he huskily whispered being things like "Water please." For several years he had great difficulty keeping straight in his mind his mother, wife, and daughter. It was as though his brain had completely scrambled the significant women in his life; he often thought his daughter was his mother or his wife, or referred to my mother by my sister's name. He lacked the strength to move the most minor of muscles, so he had to be helped even to scratch his ear. Then, three days before his death, there was an amazing event. He spontaneously sat bolt upright in bed, vigorously reached out his arms, and with the full-bodied voice of a forty-year-old, called my mother's name: "Agnes, Agnes, over here." Then he fell back into his bed as if in a coma. This was startling, for no one had heard his voice this strong or seen his physical movements this bold or forthright for many years. This story reminded me of the many people who, after being clinically dead and then revived, report that they were being assisted in the passage to the other side by spirits of relatives and friends who came to greet them.

## *Returning to the Beginning*

I began my journey wanting to know why it is so hard to find "a sense of home" in this life. I found that I am most "at home" in this world, and in my heart, when I acknowledge that this life is but a wayside stop, that my essence is far more than this flesh and these bones. Since affirming my spiritual homelessness, I have no longer needed to search for a home anymore. The feeling that no place feels like home is difficult, but it is the sharp edge of a dull ache affecting us all. When we affirm the ways we do not feel at home, we find the common bond that exists among us all and paradoxically discover how to be at home wherever we are. We do not feel at home here because this is not our home. Our spirits belong to some other place, and our sojourn in these earthly bodies is merely a passage.

There is a beautiful story of a young boy that captures this perfectly. Upon the birth of his brother, this lad asked his parents if he could have some time alone with the baby. Initially his parents were too preoccupied to attend to his request, but he was persistent. Eventually they got the message, so his mother and father left the nursery to give him the privacy he wanted. However, their curiosity was too much for them and they listened in on the baby monitor. This was what they heard their five-year-old say. He pulled himself close to his baby brother's face and with the most soulful of tones, pleaded, "Please tell me what God is like. I am beginning to forget. Please tell me what it is like to be at home."[23]

This wee boy said it all. By accepting that our earthly existence is but a wayside pause on our trip back to the place from whence we have come, we feel more at home within our emotional and communal selves. *Home is a condition of the spirit.* When we realize that truth, which emerges only from the depths of the vulnerable heart, it is also evident that:

Every step we take is upon hallowed ground,
Every task we do is the Lord's work,
Every outstretched hand offered in love is the hand
    of God,
Every breath we take is spirit filled,
Every moment we live is pregnant with transformative
    possibility.

> *For thee have I waited all the day long,*
> *for the coming of thy goodness, Lord.*
>
> Psalm 25:5

# Notes

1. The Power Laboratory was created by Barry Oshry and Fritz Steel. See Barry Oshry, *Power and Position* (Boston: Power and Systems, 1977), and K. K. Smith, *Groups in Conflict: Prisons in Disguise* (Dubuque: Kendall-Hunt, 1982).

2. See Daniel Halpern, ed., *Holy Fire: Nine Visionary Poets and the Quest for Enlightenment* (New York: HarperPerennial, 1994), 10.

3. Henri J. M Nouwen, *Lifesigns: Intimacy, Fecundity, and Ecstasy in Christian Perspective* (New York: Doubleday Image, 1986), 27.

4. Ibid., 29.

5. Henri J. M. Nouwen, *The Return of the Prodigal Son: A Meditation on Fathers, Brothers, and Sons* (New York: Doubleday, 1992), 15.

6. See Roger Fisher and William Ury, *Getting to Yes: Negotiating Agreement without Giving In* (Boston: Houghton Mifflin, 1992), and Richard G. Shell, *Bargaining for Advantage: Negotiation Strategies for Reasonable People* (New York: Bantam, 1999).

7. See Barry Oshry, *Power and Position;* Barry Oshry, *Middle Power* (Boston: Power and Systems, 1980); Barry Oshry, *Leading Systems: Lessons from the Power Lab* (San Francisco: Berrett-Kohler, 1999); and Kenwyn K. Smith, *Groups in Conflict.*

8. The material for this book came from thousands of pages of documents. Chapters 2 and 3 are constructed from the notes generated by the staff who served as anthropologists at Beacon Hill and Fellowship Farm. The material for chapters 5 through 9 came from students' papers, videotapes of group dynamics sessions, discussions during the review periods following the Labs, and various conversations held with participants after the course was concluded.

9. For a full discussion of this idea see Seymour B. Sarason, *The Creation of Settings and the Future Societies* (San Francisco: Jossey-Bass, 1972), and Kenwyn K. Smith and David N. Berg, *Paradoxes of Group Life* (San Francisco: Jossey-Bass, 1987).

10. For a full description of another retreat similar to Beacon Hill, see the Montville section of Kenwyn K. Smith, *Groups in Conflict.*

11. From the movie *Crocodile Dundee* when Mick Dundee explains how the Australian Aborigine views himself as just a temporary steward of the land he occupies.

12. The poet David Whyte has a discussion of this in his book *The Heart Aroused* (New York: Doubleday, 1994), 73–115.

13. Otto Rank has a wonderful discussion about how uniqueness and commonness, while being each other's opposites, are also each other's complements. See Otto Rank, *Will Therapy and Truth and Reality* (New York: Knopf, 1945), 46–59.

14. I am using this term to capture the belief that we can only be more when we have more: a bigger house, a larger organization, more possessions, an expanding sphere of influence, etc.

15. I have invented this term to represent the kind of public policy thinking that has risen once more since the World Trade Center attacks, where one nation insists that God is on our side in the fight against those forces deemed as evil; this is only one step short of evoking the motif of the crusades, which justifies the killing of anyone not deemed to be on our side.

16. Ronald D. Laing, *The Politics of the Family* (New York: Vintage, 1969), 96.

17. Ibid. For a full explanation of these clinical concepts see Anthony Storr, *The Integrity of the Personality* (Harmondsworth, England: Penguin, 1963), 76–114.

18. See Derrick Bell, *Faces at the Bottom of the Well: The Permanence of Racism* (New York: Basic Books, 1992). This contains an eloquent and desolate lament about how racism has become a permanent feature of the American landscape.

19. In W. E. B. Du Bois, *The Souls of Black Folk* in *Three Negro Classics* (New York: Avalon Books, 1965); originally published in 1903.

20. Upon my father's death in 1995, I came across a shoebox full of the letters he wrote to his family between 1932 and 1949, the years he lived in China. His mother had gathered these and placed them in a box that my dad retrieved upon her death in the 1960s. And I retrieved them upon my dad's death. When I opened them they were being examined for the first time in over forty years. His letters chronicled the rise of Mao Dedong and the struggle between the Chiang Kai-shek military regime and the emerging communist revolution.

21. This is the painting represented on the cover of this book.

22. "Be Like the Bird" by Victor Hugo, first translated into English in the late 1800s and appearing in *The Works of Victor Hugo*, vols. 5–7, *Poems* (Boston: Colonial Press), and later in another version of the *Works of Victor*

*Hugo,* 10 vols., translated by various authors (New York and Philadelphia: Nottingham Society, 1907). This poem was included in Michael Harrison, *Splinters: A Book of Very Short Poems* (Oxford: Oxford University Press, 1989). In recent years this poem has been in the public domain (it can be found on the Internet and on posters). However, when my mother first sent it to me, three decades ago, it was relatively unknown.

23. Dr. R. Maurice Boyd told this story in his sermon "Corridors of Light" preached at New York Avenue Presbyterian Church, September 8, 1991.

*Another book by Kenwyn K. Smith,*
*published by The Pilgrim Press:*

## MANNA in the Wilderness of AIDS
### *Ten Lessons in Abundance*

This is the true story of seven motivated people from a church in Philadelphia. Their modest initiative to serve food to AIDS victims was transformed into a vibrant nonprofit interfaith organization aptly named MANNA (Metropolitan AIDS Neighborhood Nutrition Alliance) — and resulted in the revitalization of their community, themselves, and their church. Kenwyn K. Smith was the first chair of MANNA's board of directors, serving from 1990 to 1996. The MANNA project in Philadelphia is a recipient of the Presbyterian Church (U.S.A.) Bicentennial Funds.

ISBN 0-8298-1458-2
Paper, 214 pages, $17.00

To order this or any other books from
The Pilgrim Press, call or write:

**The Pilgrim Press**
**700 Prospect Avenue East**
**Cleveland, OH 44115-1100**

Phone orders: 800.537.3394
(M–F, 8:30am–4:30pm ET)
Fax orders: 216.736.2206

Please include shipping charges of $4.00 for the first book
and 75¢ for each additional book.

Or order from our web site at www.pilgrimpress.com.

Prices subject to change without notice.